STUFF WOMEN CAN'T DO:

25 Things We All Know Girls Can't Do
(But We Pretend They Can)

Authored By

Niles Mercado
Frasier Mercado

DEDICATION

This book is dedicated to

Karen Straughan

Whose groundbreaking **Anti-Feminist** research was the inspiration for this volume.

ISBN-10: 1539369102
ISBN-13: 978-1539369103

DISCLAIMERS

- Absolutely nothing in this volume is meant to constitute legal, financial, medical and certainly not relationship advice nor are the opinions presented to be considered expert opinions (although we are **completely correct**).

- In this volume, each particular detail is presented to the best of our knowledge and understanding of the Female sex. If you think any of our analysis, or review is inaccurate **please email us** and we will correct it and publish an updated edition after we verify that you aren't just a politically correct beta-male zombie (easyinputbooks@gmail.com).

- Most importantly: absolutely no portion of this mind-blowing work was written in a Starbucks.

CONTENTS

1 – WOMEN CAN'T UNDERSTAND THIS BOOK

Women can't understand this book. The reason women[1] will have difficulty understanding this book is because **they do not understand generalizations**. I will try and explain what they are as simply as I can.

A "g-e-n-e-r-a-l-i-z-a-t-i-o-n" is not turning somebody into a military General, but it is saying something that applies in a majority (or big number) of cases, but are not without exceptions[2].

Figure 1 - If You're Confused, We Understand

The reason why men know that women do not understand generalizations is because when they (men) make general comments, the most common response is to provide a few exceptions. If an answer to a general comment is, "there are exceptions", then you can tell they aren't getting it.

Lots of people have asked us "why are you writing this book. Is it just to piss people (me) off?" -No.

---

[1] And beta-males.
[2] Trying to explain this simply for the Feminists, Beta-Males and Politically Correct Zombies out there.

Mainly it's because society is living in a fantasy world, far outside of the bounds of reality.

A world cannot function this divorced from reality for long. *Men are worthless oppressors. The only thing a man is good for is holding a woman back.* We've all heard the anti-male propaganda that most take for granted.

Value is partly determined by our differences. If women can do everything a man can, then what good are men?

Equality does not mean **sameness**. This book is more equality-based than the world's view point (and certainly more equality-based than the feminist perspective).

The majority of people fully accept that society cannot function without women. We would not have the next generation; who is going to make the children?

But feminists are CONSTANTLY saying that they don't need men, men are **disposable**. Male disposability, disturbingly, is a very common discussion point. In some of the more extreme cases feminists openly talk about executing 90% of men as a solution for world peace!

In the chapters to come you are going to see a lot of things that women either can't do or just refuse to do, *as a group.*

It's not that women are inferior to men, but the things that are uniquely masculine are not appreciated. As a result, there are very elaborate sand castles in peoples' minds, over-inflating women's abilities and accomplishments, and completely ignoring and denigrating man's contributions, not to mention the lengths they go through, the dangers they put themselves in, just to make women happy.

We are living in this imaginary world, irrespective of facts, logic and reality. And nobody (until now) wants to rock the boat, because some woman's feelings might get hurt.

This book is really about understanding and appreciating men. Their accomplishments and what they can uniquely do. And, yes, we are going to accomplish this by detailing the things women simply can't do.

Men and women are different and the differences are largely NOT a "social construct" but are differences that are mimicked throughout the mammalian order of species. This may seem a very basic notion, but through propaganda this basic fact has joined the long lists of things you are not allowed to talk about.

ASPIRATION IS NOT REALITY

We were first inspired to create this book after reading the hilarious volume that taught the world what white people like. But, the aptly-titled book "Stuff White People Like" was not really about **all** white people. It was really about **white liberals living in Metropolitan areas**.

This book is NOT about **all** women. It can't be. We don't KNOW all women! But more importantly than that there are good women that appreciate the different strengths of each sex and there are the other women that don't. This book is primarily about the latter.

In fact, all women can take this book as an inspiration, almost as a dare to be proved wrong - with actions, instead of outrage. Show the world you're not *that* kind of woman. Even if you are a go-go career woman, that thinks that men have no unique strengths, try and react in a positive way to what we are saying.

Especially in the case of inventions (see Chapter 10). Let this be your battle cry on your way to accomplishment and greatness. More power to you; let spite be your muse.

Please note, this book cannot be proved wrong by listing exceptions. We are making general comments here (duh).

This book is not directed to all women. Really this is directed to the women who do not appreciate men and do not acknowledge the uniqueness of men.

The women in our personal lives **loved the concept of this book** and have encouraged us to move forward with it. There is a difference between good women and women who have a very twisted perception of the "genders".[3]

It is not necessarily our goal to piss anybody off in the making of this, but the fact that the title of the book, or the title of any of the chapters can piss anybody off to the extent that it probably will is more than enough validation for why we wanted to write this book in the first place.

Think of this book as an easy way to get people's attention combined with being a sly mechanism to actually discuss some of the real world problems men and women are facing. We present the facts as we see them, convenient or otherwise. It is up to you to consider what we are saying. If you disagree please **send us actual facts** that prove what we are saying is **generally false** (not specific exceptions). Or you could just virtue signal and smear us in the Amazon reviews and in the blogosphere. I wish I could bet on which one will happen more…

Publisher's Email: easyinputbooks@gmail.com

---

[3] As a side note "genders" is not a thing. The term "gender" used to be confined to language, as in this is the "masculine" tense, "feminine tense", "neutral tense", etc. The term within biology has always been "sex", as in Male or Female. Sex is essentially completely binary within biology, with some species having both and asexual species having none. Either way biology was binary and used the term sex and gender was a greyer area that applied to speech conjugation.

Injecting the term "gender" when talking about people's sex was just a sly way to get people to ignore their biological identification. Now NYC says there are 31 different genders and addressing someone incorrectly can get your business sued. Yay! I guess we should save that for a book about gays, Stuff Gays Can't Do. 1) Have children with their sexual partners… I think this might get too depressing, never mind, pretend this book has no footnotes.

2 – WOMEN CAN'T DO SPORTS

Women can't play sports. Period. To fully understand what we mean here, obviously a woman can engage in a sport at some time and place.

What we really mean here is to just point out the fact that the **WNBA** is (as are other female sports leagues) basically **equivalent to the Special Olympics.** Meaning that in order for them to have their individual achievements they need to exclude the players that can beat them.

That is the purpose of the Special Olympics. It is to provide self-esteem. The Special Olympics (which I have volunteered at repeatedly) is meant to build up the participants and make them feel good about participating in a competition where they have a chance of winning.

The same goes for the WNBA; Obviously if they let the NBA players play against them, none of them would be winning or even make the team.

Figure 2 - Looks Kind of Like a Soccer Ball, But Something Isn't Right

And this is a fact that is **so plainly in front of everyone** but not mentioned. Everyone is aware of it, though nobody is allowed to talk about it.

When the WNBA is brought up, it is always used to criticize men for not giving it the respect that it is due. Compared to what? Compared to the NBA? Sure, the WNBA doesn't get THAT much respect. People give the NBA a lot more credence, because basically men can run faster, jump higher and jump farther. They are stronger and faster. These are not sexist claims; instead, these are physiological certainties.

Thus, when you watch the NBA you are seeing **the best** basketball players in the world, **bar none.** Therefore, it deservedly gets much more respect.

Obviously you could find some **individual man** who cannot run as fast as some **individual woman,** but that is completely meaningless as we are talking about generalizations (see Chapter 1).

Also, between the world's best male players and the world's best female players, there is hardly anything that can be considered a sport in which the women would consistently beat the men. The reverse is true in almost every case.

Even in the Olympics, things like track and field are not unisex. There is no other real reason why these things would be separated by gender. Track and Field also gives very finite results regarding their aptitude. You can see how fast men and women can run, how high or far men and women can jump, etc. That is probably one reason there are not too many professional female athletes, or sports with a strong fan base for the female participants.

The greatest exception would have to be tennis. There are female tennis players that are famous the world over, and people do watch women's tennis. Even in this case, the best women's tennis player is not going to beat the best men's tennis player: Federer beats Serena Williams.

The one example that ALWAYS gets propped up by women's rights groups as an example of women's supremacy and dominance over men is Billy Gene King defeating Bobby Riggs.

The truth is that she was at the top of her career, in her prime beating a very old man who had been retired from tennis for a very long time. Had she played against the top male tennis player at the time she would have lost handedly, which is why she didn't do that.

Yet, somehow this event is taught and re-taught; TV movies are made about this event, where women are shown watching across America, their mouths agape, little girls looking on, thinking to themselves, "I can achieve so much more now with this newfound inspiration." Meanwhile it was just a young professional female player beating a very old man with gambling debts.

Obviously Serena Williams can beat us, we are not tennis players. But the best male player in any sport, can beat the best female player in any sport, without exception. Even in tennis; just look at the speed of their serves.

Men DO respect certain women's sports. If you're wondering why women's tennis is so much more popular than the WNBA, women's tennis is DIFFERENT than men's.

They dress different, **they dress as women**. Or with A League of Their Own, with female baseball, while men were fighting in World War II, they **dressed and acted like women**. Where women are trying to BE boys is where men will reject it, en masse.

Female figure skating and gymnastics (two female sports that ACTUALLY garner an audience the world over) are two prime examples of this **intact femininity** at play.

If the WNBA wants to achieve some actual relevance they will follow their figure-skating and tennis-playing sisters and stop dressing up as boys. This just shows you how much of a fantasy world most people are living in.

Imagine someone had come to me and said "do you think men will watch a bunch of women in drag, trying pass for men playing basketball?"

I would have been able to clearly tell them "um, no, if they want to see that they will just watch real men playing basketball, but if they dress and even act like women then your league has a chance because then they will have differentiated themselves from the NBA".

I wouldn't have even had to think about that because I am not a hypnotized politically-correct zombie.

It should also be noted that women, overall, do not CARE about sports, nor do they want to play it as much, or on the same level as men do.   This is why there is so much government financing of women's sports.

Title 9 was passed, requiring public schools and state sponsored universities to offer just as much female athletics programs as male. They struggle year after year to fill the programs with women who WANT to play them.

This lost cause has been in full effect since the late 1970s.   They have even had to cancel successful men's programs in order to push a rope, propping up this lie that men and women are the same, that their desire to play sports (regardless of ability) is identical.

As a society we should really ask ourselves: why are we so eager to cram men and women into a homogenous uni-mold?   What is so bad about men and women pursuing different things in life with their own unique achievements?

3 – WOMEN CAN'T PAY TAXES

Sure, an individual woman might pay taxes, but as a group women do not pay taxes. As a group, women are net tax **receivers**, while men are (as a group) net tax **payers**.

What that means fundamentally is that women consume more in direct government services (*not even counting roads and such*) **than they will ever pay in taxes**. Put in that perspective, you can begin to understand why women would be more in favor of spending and taxation.

Men, on the other hand, tend to want a smaller government, less taxes; they are not benefiting (directly, anyways) from taxation and government programs. The government then simply amounts to a **forceful transfer of wealth from men to women**. Men get virtually nothing in return in this arrangement.

Figure 3 - As a Group, Women Are Net Tax RECEIVERS

This fact has massive implications as it relates to how government is run, the types of programs that get voted for.

As a group, women are simply voting for what to do with men's money. Therefore, they are always going to want to do more and more things with more and more tax dollars.

It's sort of like a backwards home owner's association (HOA). Normally only the people who own homes vote in a home owner's association because they are the ones paying the fees. Whereas people lying in the street, sleeping in parks, they don't get a vote in the home owners association because they are not paying those fees. If you did give them a vote, what would happen to that association?

What would happen is money would be diverted to the parks, the policies of the parks would change so the homeless could have nicer benches, air conditioned areas available to everybody.

In other words, if you give the people who are not paying the right to vote, they are always going to want more from the people who ARE paying.

Now you understand the out-of-control spending and mounting national debt plaguing ever western democracy that gave women the right to vote a century or so ago.

Politicians just can't say no to women who, in general, are asking NOT what they can do for their country but what their country can do for THEM.

Social programs are only part of the picture. Let's take a look at one of America's favorite modern myths.

4 – WOMEN CAN'T BE INDEPENDENT

There is a widely held myth that most traditional women in history were **dependent** on men but that the **"modern" woman is independent**.

Of course nothing could be further from the truth. It would be more accurate to say that traditionally dependent men and women were in symbiotic interdependence (in traditional society) and modern women are the parasitically dependent ones today.

The whole practice of Feminism amounts to, little more than, lobbying the government to shake down men and forcibly transfer resources from men to woman.

The reality is that an individual woman can be independent but, as a group, resources need to flow from men to women in order for the species to continue.

Traditional women would provide value as wives, mothers, domestic engineers, increasing the family's reputation through charity/volunteer work and usually stretching the family budget. The modern western woman would prefer to get what she needs from men without providing anything in return.

Lower class women get welfare, food stamps, etc. Middle class women get alimony, government jobs, scholarships and grants while **upper class women** receive huge divorce settlements and preferential government contracts.

Using the **magic of government force**, these women provide nothing but votes for the political class in return. **Billions upon billions are transferred** every year this way and each year more women jump on the bandwagon. I mean if someone paid you to NOT do your current job, wouldn't you quit?

How did this myth originate and perpetrate? Decades worth of TV shows, movies and music has instilled this myth into our perceived reality.

Starting with the 1970s, with shows like "The Mary Tyler Moore Show". The opening theme triumphantly exclaimed, "You're gonna make it on your own." The creators wanted her to be divorced, the network wanted her as a widow. They met in the middle with her breaking up an engagement.

A single woman was working in a man's world, glorifying single woman-hood long into her thirties (the decade when most women become infertile). It should be noted that the REAL Mary Tyler Moore was happily married <u>during the entire run of the show</u>. That in itself is a huge deception. They needed a woman who had the benefit of the love, sense of security, and support provided by a husband to project the image of a single woman happily making it on her own!

The 70s also ushered in songs like "Sisters Are Doin' It For Themselves." If the "IT" in the song refers to making enough money to support themselves, they are not. The amount that transfers in the form of Social Programs, Obamacare and food stamps is roughly the same amount as the budget deficit. In other words, there could be a balanced budget if the government wasn't taking money from men and giving it to women. Thanks a lot Mary Tyler Moore! That's another fine mess you've gotten us into.

5 – WOMEN CAN'T BE FUNNY

In January of 2007, Vanity Fair published an article written by Christopher Hitchens. Before we get ahead of ourselves, let's clarify a few things for our younger readers: Christopher Hitchens was an editorial journalist who achieved some notoriety writing about atheism (pro).

He was also a featured writer for Vanity Fair. Vanity Fair is a monthly American magazine that explores entertainment, culture, fashion and politics. Magazines are collections of articles and pictures that are published periodically and printed on paper. Paper is a wood based material your parents used to record sentences.

Hitchens' article and its four-word title made people's heads explode, sparking a never-ending social justice debate for the ages. The article was titled "WHY WOMEN AREN'T FUNNY."

Those four words sent shock waves reverberating throughout the comedy industry as the blogosphere and media at large tripped over themselves to refute Hitchens' articles in rather lame and predictable ways.

Cracked (which is still a thing) published an article titled "4 Ways We're **Programmed to Think** Women Aren't Funny"

The Guardian asked the question, "Why Do People **BELIEVE** Women Aren't Funny?".

Then there was the Atlantic article entitled "Why Men Don't **Like** Funny Women", putting the comedy gap at men's doorsteps with the subtitle, "Why people tend to **appreciate** men's humor much more than women's."

Just as surprising as the "Why Women Aren't Funny" title and content, was its source. After all Christopher Hitchens was not the right-leaning Archie Bunker style blow-hard from whom one would expect to hear such proclamations. The same goes for the left leaning, "socially conscious" Vanity Fair.

So what gives? How did this controversial article slip past the goalie? Was Hitchens even serious? He couldn't be, right? I mean, women ARE funny. Aren't they?

Before we get into the (humorless) feminist backlash, or whether Hitchens' article holds water, let's first consider what he ACTUALLY said. The truth is the article's thesis is a bit more reasonable than its 4-word title might suggest. Consider a few excerpts:

> *"This is not to say that women are humorless, or cannot make great wits and comedians."*

But rather-

> *"Why are men, taken on average and as a whole, funnier than women?"*

Then offers this as a possible explanation:

> *"The chief task in life that a man has to perform is that of impressing the opposite sex... An average man has just one, outside chance: he had better be able to make the lady laugh."*

In other words, Hitchens was saying that ON AVERAGE men are funnier than women because women are already so attractive to men. If men want to gain the affection of the opposite sex (for sex), they better learn to impress them with a good sense of humor. Or, put another way by female humorist Fran Leibowitz, "The cultural values are male; for a woman to say a man is funny is the equivalent of a man saying that a woman is pretty."

Even if you disagree with Christopher Hitchens and his article, you have to admit that it's not exactly the misogynistic diatribe one would expect. Hitchens' article was so reasonable, in fact, that even those who tried to refute it could not help but (inadvertently) agree with his premise.

Take Peter McGraw and Joel Warner article in Slate called "No, Men are not funnier than women":

> *"In the course of researching our book, we met with humorists all over the world—and in* **MOST CASES***, those humorists were* **MALE***. In Los Angeles, the* **VAST MAJORITY** *of the stand-up comedians we spoke to were* **MEN***. When we got a behind-the-scenes look at the New Yorker cartoon process in Manhattan,* **NEARLY ALL THE CARTOONISTS WERE MEN***. And when we visited a comedy training school in Tokyo, which is essentially mandatory for would-be Japanese comedians, there were a* **total of two women** *in* **both 60-student classes** *we sat in on."* (emphasis ours)

WHAT? Did they just say there were more male comedians than female? Michèle A'Court did the same thing in her article in the Guardian:

> *"Why are there so few women comedians? This is a global phenomenon and, after being forced to think about it for two decades, I believe there are three related reasons."*

What reason do they provide for this humor gap? Slate

has this to say:

> *"That said, studies have found differences in the way men and women talk about humor in the context of dating and mating. In 2011, researchers analyzed more than 250 online dating profiles posted by people in London and several Canadian cities. They found that men were nearly twice as likely to boast of their humor-production abilities ('I'm an aspiring stand-up comic'), while women were nearly twice as likely to be looking for a humor producer ('I want someone who can make me giggle')."*

> *"The discrepancy could be linked to humor's evolutionary origins. A sense of humor in men could be seen as a sign of intelligence, social desirability, and overall genetic fitness. So guys might have an incentive to show off their comedy chops, while women are incentivized to be on the lookout for the funniest possible mate. According to evolutionary psychology, male mating goals are different: Men theoretically look for a healthy mate—i.e., someone young, healthy, and attractive—before they look for signs of intellect and social intelligence, so a woman's sense of humor would matter less."*

Wait, what? Did Slate just say the same exact thing Hitchens said, but with different words and a misleading title?

What about that Cracked article discussing the 4 Ways We're Programmed to Think Women Aren't Funny? Number 3 is "Humor Gets Men Laid":

> *"When a woman laughs at a joke, the reward center of her brain lights up like crazy. The reward center is the part of your brain that makes you feel good when you eat chocolate or have sex or key your ex's car. So making a woman laugh results in a hugely pleasurable experience for her, which can lead to an even more pleasurable experience for you both."*

How come these rebuttal articles can't help but agree with the article they are supposed to be rebutting? Could it be that Hitchens' premise actually holds some water, and that this might be the reason it was written in the first place and subsequently struck such a sensitive chord?

Consider the following: For thousands of years, men have had to prove their ability to gain resources for women in order for them to survive genetically. Most of the qualities women say they are looking for in men relate back to that ability. "I want a guy that can make me laugh" is really code for wanting a man that is intelligent and emotionally and situationally aware enough to succeed in the marketplace.

So, men have had centuries developing their ability to make women and others laugh (in a non-clownish way that preserves their social status). By contrast, men have been primarily concerned with fertility markers and, to a lesser extent, practicality and soundness of mind.

Good traits, but none of them require the women to be funny. Also remember that historically women were twice as likely to pass their genes on to the next generation (geneticists claim that we come from twice as many women as men) so the pressure to perform just wasn't there.

Maybe you agree with this premise; maybe you don't. Okay... SO WHAT!?!?!? What I find really sad about the Funny Women debate is how adverse people are to freeness of thought, debate, discussion, inference and observation. Each article can't help but acknowledge "humor gap" phenomenon, that the comedy industry, from stand up, to sketch comedy writing and sitcoms are all dominated by men.

They each give their own explanation for this irrefutable imbalance, yet when Christopher Hitchens did this, it inspired never ending vitriol and bitterness.

One of the most common sentiments to be expressed in these rebuttal articles is that we should JUST STOP TALKING ABOUT THIS.

This debate has raged on far too long. The very suggestion that men are funnier is misogynistic, sexist and "obviously" unfounded. Female comedians bemoan even being asked about this disparity.

> "I don't ever want to answer this question again. It makes me tired."
> Michèle A'Court - The Guardian

The Independent inquired with their article titled, "Can we now stop asking if women are as funny as men?"

E Online published this article: "Why "Tina Fey Will No Longer Answer the Question 'Are Women Funny?'"

Kelly Martinek commanded her Michigan Daily readers with her article titled, "Stop Saying Women Aren't Funny".

So there you have it. Don't observe the world around you. Don't voice those observations because they could hurt people's feelings. Don't make inferences based on those observations to better understand the world around you. And this is supposed to make people respect women? If you can't talk frankly about the differences between people it means you don't respect them to be mature enough to handle it.

Maybe we shouldn't let the offended social justice warriors decide what we're allowed to observe and discuss. We leave you with this Hitchens meme that sums it up nicely:

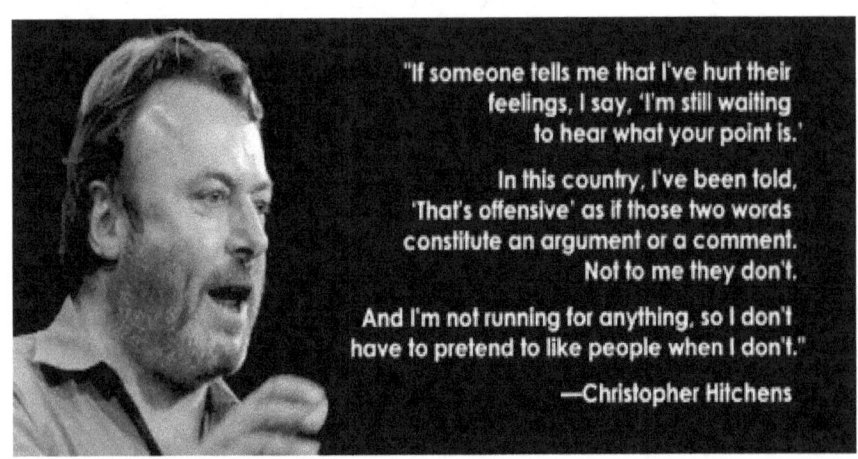

"If someone tells me that I've hurt their feelings, I say, 'I'm still waiting to hear what your point is.'

In this country, I've been told, 'That's offensive' as if those two words constitute an argument or a comment. Not to me they don't.

And I'm not running for anything, so I don't have to pretend to like people when I don't."

—Christopher Hitchens

6 – WOMEN CAN'T DESERVE 100 CENTS (ON THE $)

We have all heard the braindead complaint about women earning "82 cents on the dollar".

Of course that figure could not be more misleading [see https://www.youtube.com/watch?v=1oqyrflOQFc].

There really IS NO WAGE GAP! Or only in the least meaningful way is there a wage gap because women make all of these different life choices.

They work part time, less hours, less overtime but that is a whole subject for another chapter (see Chapter 13).

The types of careers they choose are more about connecting with animals or humans (customer service); those jobs just don't pay as much as the hard sciences, finance, dirty jobs and engineering.

The following is kind of an "a priori" argument[4], in other words it can be proven logically without the need for specific data (but then we link you to an article with a whole bunch of data).

If you just think how **impossible** it is to have an 18 percent wage gap based off of discrimination you quickly realize

---

[4] http://www.merriam-webster.com/dictionary/a%20priori

how ridiculous it is. The reason is that if you have anything close to a free market, companies will sometimes enter a field and obliterate competition based on their ability to operate at a **1 to 2 percentage point margin** advantage.

With 2 percent increased efficiency, they can **obliterate their competition**. So, if we're saying that labor, which in America's economy is one of the top 2 expenses, if we are saying that companies in general are undervaluing women by 18 percentage points, that would quickly be rectified by entrepreneurs that would take advantage of that fact.

They would go, *"oh look, there is all this female talent being underpaid. Instead of 18 cents less on the dollar, let's pay them 14 cents less, or 10 cents less".*

Companies would **continue to bid up their salaries** until the margin of difference all but disappeared. These other companies with higher wages for their female employees would then benefit because they would have all these employees who were super proficient, more proficient than the competition that was refusing to pay them a fair wage.

Different forms of discrimination have been tried in the past, but for the same reason, didn't last. Just think about how Jews[5] had to leave New York, to create Hollywood.

One of the reasons you have so many movie studios being run by Jews (and initially started by Jews) was BECAUSE of discrimination. That did not prevent success among a minority group; instead it may have spurred it on.

SIDE NOTE: *The market abhors irrational decision making. Governments on the other hand have enforced discrimination repeatedly throughout history.*

A lot of things that we think of in the past as

---

[5] For the Politically Correct Zombies (not to mention anti-Zionist conspiracy theorists) I will disclose that the writers of this book are each half Jewish (ethnically). Hopefully now you won't cringe for the rest of the chapter when you read "Jew" (it's not a four letter word people)!

discrimination, actually had government involvement. For example, we are all familiar with the story of Rosa Parks, who refused to get up from her seat in the front of the bus. That policy was instituted by the local government, not the marketplace. The bus company did not want to institute this policy. It was there by law.

In fact, we see that when you compare wages between men and women in similar industries with similar work experience there is no wage gap.

When you "normalize the data" (which just means comparing apples to apples) men and women almost always make the same amount (sometimes women make 1% more than the men and vice versa).

But this is probably not worth arguing about. According to Scott Adams, the creator of **Dilbert**, men should save their energy something other than dispelling the 80 cents-on-the-dollar nonsense:

> *"The reality is that **women are treated differently by society for exactly the same reason that children and the mentally handicapped are treated differently**. It's just easier this way for everyone. You don't argue with a four-year old about why he shouldn't eat candy for dinner. You don't punch a mentally handicapped guy even if he punches you first. And you **don't argue when a woman tells you she's only making 80 cents** to your dollar. It's the path of least resistance. You **save your energy for more important battles**."*[6]

Further Reading:

Forbes: It's Time That We End the Equal Pay Myth
http://www.forbes.com/sites/realspin/2012/04/16/its-time-that-we-end-the-equal-pay-myth/

---

[6] http://blog.dilbert.com/post/102881506316/im-a-what and (***emphasis*** ours)

7 – WOMEN CAN'T DO DANGEROUS JOBS

Before the great recession, 93% of workplace deaths befell men. That's right, while women and their political harem masters are whining about a totally rational 18 cent Gender Wage Gap you haven't heard a thing about the much larger and more perilous **Gender Death Gap**.

In fact, the press didn't care about workplace deaths until the Great Recession put so many men out of work that less men were able to have stuff fall on them and kill them. Why did they care when less men died? Was this to celebrate this silver lining of the recession? Hardly!

It was because less men dying meant that the PERCENTAGE of workplace deaths that befell women rose from 7% to a still paltry 13%. So all the articles cared about was the fact that AS A PERCENTAGE female deaths had almost doubled (even though the female deaths remained relatively constant).

It was branded as a public health crisis putting women in peril. Why didn't anyone care about the 87% (or the original 93%) of men making up workplace deaths? That leads us to the next thing women can't do (see next chapter).

Take a look at the table below detailing the deadliest jobs and the percentage of the workers that are male and consider the following:

- If you are a woman reading this, think to yourself: do you have any of these jobs? Do you know any woman with these jobs? If so would you consider them exceptions or representative of the women that you are familiar with?

- If you feel appalled about the Gender Death Gap, feel free to personally do something about it and obtain one of these jobs. In the very least find a man doing one of these jobs and let them know how much you appreciate him putting his life on the line. Chances are you won't do this last part because of the next thing women can't do.

Top Ten Most Dangerous US Occupations and Percent Male, 2013

Rank	Occupation	Fatal Injury Rate per 100,000 workers	Percent Male
1	Logging Workers	91.3	97.9%
2	Fishers	75.0	100.0%
3	Aircraft Pilots	50.6	94.5%
4	Extraction Workers	46.9	97.9%
5	Roofers	38.7	99.3%
6	Refuse Collectors	33.0	95.2%
7	Mining Machine Operators	26.9	95.0%
8	Truck Drivers	22.0	94.8%
9	Farmers and Ranchers	21.8	74.7%
10	Electrical Power-Line Workers	21.5	98.9%

Source : Bureau of Labor Statistics, Census of Fatal Occupational Injuries

8 – WOMEN CAN'T HAVE EMPATHY FOR MEN

Women can't seem to care when men complain, cry or even get raped. Most American women have trouble mustering up even the smallest hints of empathy for men.

Have you ever heard a woman complain that men don't express their feelings? I wonder why that is. Could it be that when men do express their feelings they get accused of **mansplaining** (*even though feminism is little more than non-stop chicksplaining*).

Even more foundational is the fact that study after study has confirmed that mothers are much less likely to pick up or respond to a crying male baby than a crying female baby (more on this in a bit). Then male children are more likely to be abused by their mothers than their sisters.

Then these boys get to public school that is completely tailored to the needs of girls and when they don't fall inline their (mostly female) teachers recommend they get put on psychotropic drugs.

Then they come home from school and watch TV where every adult male is made to look like an idiot (especially husband-providers). Raymond, King of Queens, Tim Allen, Family Guy, Al Bundy, Homer Simpson and every single Disney TV father figure (since Scrooge McDuck I would say) **all** follow this template.

Then they get to college and are **treated as potential rapists** and are made to sit through inane rape awareness classes.

If they express their opinions, they need to first issue trigger warnings and make sure they aren't in a "safe space" which is really a safe space *for anti-male hatred*.

So after being neglected, abused, drugged, told by TV that their preferences are unimportant, stupid or worse, they are treated like a pre-criminal – mostly by the hands of women. After all that they are a little hesitant to express themselves. Big surprise!

Then, if the male child survives all this, when they get into the workplace if they talk, to even fellow men, in a normal male manner someone overhearing can get offended and run to the HR department (*which is like a little kid running to complain to mom*).

Then if men have any difficulty in their lives they are **derided openly** in nearly every form of media.

Is a man having some existential questions after 15 years of marriage to a feminist harpy who is treating him like garbage? If that marriage falls apart and he ends up marrying someone younger is there any examination of the ex-wife and her treatment of him? Is there any sympathy for the mess that man is living through? No, because let's just all make fun of the man having a **Midlife Crisis**.

Has reduced economic performance led a man to live in an underused part of his parents' house (like the basement) temporarily while he saves money and rebuilds his income? Well, he is just a loser **living in his mother's basement** (*why is it always referred to as his "mother's" basement anyway*).

Is a man being domestically **abused by his female partner?** Look at that loser that lets himself get slapped around by his woman!

In fairness that last one rarely gets acknowledged because domestic violence is supposed to be only something men do to women.

The reality is that the majority of domestic violence incidents are physically instigated by the woman[7].

This is one of the reasons why lesbian relationships have such a high level of domestic violence[8] – because you have two women, each of which would be more likely than their male counterparts to commit domestic violence if they were in heterosexual relationships.

---

[7] http://www.independent.co.uk/news/uk/home-news/women-are-more-violent-says-study-622388.html

[8] http://www.advocate.com/crime/2014/09/04/2-studies-prove-domestic-violence-lgbt-issue

Now let me just say I have never been a huge fan of Glen Beck (even more so since the Dorito face stunt he pulled).

That said, it was something to watch as he cried on air and instead of concern about what upset him or his psychological well-being and stability everyone piled on insults.

A man crying! What can be more ridiculous? Same thing with Boehner and as we said infant boys. Feminist T-Shirts and coffee mugs abound with the slogan "I drink male tears".

When Hillary teared up a bit it actually helped her numbers because her "vulnerability" was viewed as relatable and humanizing.

As we said before, women (and men) are much less likely to pick up a boy crying in a crib than a girl. They have different ways of measuring this, but essentially they are about three times (3x) as responsive to a baby girl crying than a baby boy.

That may help put into context the whole trope about men not wanting to express their feelings. It may come from a long string of women not caring when men cry, or about male complaints, or men being upset. Starting from being a baby, parents just don't care as much about them. Perhaps this is just good training for the real world.

When they go to school, most of their teachers are women, who are given little to no training on how to deal with boys, or have empathy towards them, since they were never a boy.

The whole curriculum is centered around the needs of girls, which may explain why girls are doing so much better academically. The literature requirements are geared towards stuff women care about (*stories about people expressing their feelings are given precedent over action/plot related stories that boys respond to*).

From the school yard, a boy who cries is a pariah who can easily be picked on. On the other hand, a lot gets done because of girls' tears, in relationships, the workplace, et. When a girl cries, some wrong has been done, as in "Look what you've done. You made a girl cry." Judge, jury and executioner resides in a woman's tears.

Part of women's inability to empathize with me is the fact that **women can't seem to care when men get raped**.

The CDC redid the way they did their surveys. 2013 was the first time that raping men became a crime (officially). There were other charges, like forced sodomy, but raping men wasn't an actual crime.

Envelopment, which is when a woman rapes a man[9], because she envelops the man's you-know-what. They found out that this is a real thing that happens, and started doing victimization surveys to find out how often this occurs.

It turns out that outside of prison, men are raped almost as much as women. Only 20-30 percent of the time is it by other men. The other time it is by women, usually larger women. It is hard for us to wrap our heads around that, because it is such a foreign thought, because **nobody cares about men being raped**.

The only exception that people are aware of is men being raped in prison. The only reason you're allowed to know about that is that they are being raped by other men, which cancels it out in these people's heads (feminists, etc.)

If you think about it, a false accusation of rape is in a sense worse than rape itself, because a wrongfully convicted man falsely accused of rape can himself be continuously raped inside the prison walls.

And yet, false rape accusations are almost NEVER prosecuted in our court system. Till the end, female false rape accusers are still cajoled... sympathetic excuses given for how they were *confused* or *pressured* into their false accusations.

---

[9] Which, by the way, 40% of all rapists are women (article cites FBI and CDC data): http://www.independent.co.uk/news/uk/home-news/women-are-more-violent-says-study-622388.html

9 – WOMEN CAN'T HANDLE FREE SPEECH

What are safe spaces and trigger warnings? Nothing more than the opposite of free speech.

Now that women dominate college campuses they are shutting down dialogue that they don't agree with. It should be noted that universities have been around for centuries and, while they were dominated by men, students would just hash out their differences with debates, evidence-based writing, and ultimately acceptance of inherent differences (at least when it came to ideas).

Now that women have taken over, why don't they just use logic and reason? I'll leave that for you to decide. Modern women say "words hurt", whereas children were used to be taught that "sticks and stones will break your bones, but words will never hurt you".

So now that people have thrown out the concept of, "Sticks and stones may break my bones, but words will never hurt me", society has really lost a great deal.

Nothing can really advance in society without somebody being offended. In order to build anything, you have to chop down trees and offend nature. You couldn't have ended slavery without offending slave owners. You can't separate church and state without offending clergy members.

That inability to accept free speech is so pervasive in our society, we may not even recognize it when we see it. For example, sexual harassment in the workplace is nothing more than an inability to accept freedom of speech. We have gone to the state to legislate what can or cannot be said in the workplace, not because of male sexual harassment[10].

In the famous Michael Douglas / Demi Moore '90s workplace thriller, **Disclosure**, they reverse these roles, making it the man who is being sexually harassed in an attempt to get everybody to think that sexual harassment is a legitimate concern that effects both genders.

Now it has become very difficult for people to just ask somebody out on a date, or compliment their dress, or say they look great today.

Recently a little-known Fox News anchor (Gretchen Carlson), at the end of her contract (and career really), complained that Roger Ailes (the man who built Fox News into the cable station juggernaut it is today) was ogling her. What does ogling mean, pray tell? Ogling is another word for "looking at".

A newscaster who has cameras on her every day, as well as millions of viewers across the country is suing because a male co-worker was LOOKING at her in a way she did not care for her.

Inability to accept freedom of speech goes far beyond words and looks. At a recent protest at the University of Missouri, a man was peacefully taping the event with a video camera. A female college professor took umbrage with this; she

---

[10] We are obviously not talking about workplace rape or quid pro quo type harassment that was originally the target of sexual harassment legislation.

realized she could neither take this man on physically, nor express with words a convincing reason why he should not tape the public proceedings.

She immediately called for some males to assist her censorship. Her actual words were "I NEED SOME MUSCLE OVER HERE!"

She demanded strong, brute male force to oppress another man with his video camera for objectively recording the goings-on of a college protest.

It should be noted that "Freedom of Speech" is **only meant for offensive speech**. The only reason why there is a First Amendment in the Bill of Rights to the Constitution is for offensive speech.

Polite and non-offensive speech has ALWAYS been protected and accepted by every culture throughout the ages. If you're not shaking the apple cart, all of your speech has always been allowed.

A "safe space" has come to mean a public space (on public property or on university campuses) where you don't have to worry about hearing something you disagree with too much. That used to be reserved for people's private homes and clubs.

If you can't handle points of view you adamantly disagree with you probably need some serious therapy and not a college education (or what passes for one today). Really we aren't making fun of you with the therapy comment... we genuinely what you to get the help you need!

10 – WOMEN CAN'T INVENT STUFF

This is really a big one on the list because almost all things that **make our lives civilized** today are **inventions by men**.

Microsoft recently did an ad campaign[11] to motivate young women to become inventors; the premise of the commercial was that these girls are not being *shown* all of the examples of female inventors out there. Thus, the reason they are not inventing is that they have not been *motivated* to invent. *If women are underachieving in ANY category of life you better believe it is some evil man's fault!*

Of course nobody had to motivate men through the centuries. They were all trying to solve problems so they could get resources, so they didn't die genetically (men were historically half as likely to pass on their genes than women).

In this commercial they have to spotlight the few minor things women invented.

With the tally being around seven, the commercial is almost an exhaustive list (with maybe a few things being left out).

Seriously, it's about half of ALL of the inventions that actually matter that were created by women.

There seems to be this never-ending celebration of ANYTHING women do, and an incessant down-playing of the enormous number of things men have done and continue to do that enable the

---

[11] **Microsoft Propaganda:**
https://www.youtube.com/watch?v=Y8DBwchocvs

civilized modern world we know today.

The other myth that the commercial perpetuates is that the only reason why these girls (and perhaps you, yourself) cannot name a bunch of female inventors is because of a simple *lack of awareness* or education of female achievement. These inventors are not taught because of some patriarchal, anti-female conspiracy.

The opposite is true.   Minor accomplishments of females are lauded and aggrandized. The reason we can't name more female inventors is because their inventions are few and far between, their impact insignificant, their necessity, usually non-existent.

One of them is an adhesive used during heart surgery. If you are not trying to **prop up women's accomplishments artificially**, then the only way you would hear about the woman who invented a particular adhesive used during heart surgery would be if you had already learned all of the other minor inventions necessary to make heart surgery possible, never mind the fact that the first heart surgeries were all performed by men.

Also, think about all the other tens of thousands of types and grades of adhesives in existence, all invented by men. This is a minor contribution that they are elevating because they are trying to find female inventions.

If you are comparing that to the internal combustion engine, sewage processing, indoor plumbing, the scientific method, the assembly line, interchangeable parts etc. that is the reason these kids (and you) may not have heard about some heart surgery glue.

In order to prop up these female inventors, a few things need to happen. One, generally they focus on improvements to already existing inventions that men invented.

One example is the dishwasher, which was invented 30

years before a woman improved upon it. Her improvement required other improvements before a practical commercial product could become a reality.

There are a lot of improvements made to inventions; there might be 30 to 50 improvements in as many years before an invention looks like what we have come to know it as, but we'll only ever hear about the female incremental improvement along the way.

 # QUIET: Women Are Trying To Invent Something NOT Cookie Related

Female inventions fall into certain categories:

- Improvements on male inventions
- Things we can do without
- Minor inventions, that are basically the exception that prove the rule
- Foodstuffs that aren't really "inventions".

For instance, the fire escape was invented by a woman, but a woman did not invent stairs, modern architecture, brick and mortar, steal, welding, architecture, engineering, or any of the things that go into making a building. Nor did they invent scaffolding which is very similar to a fire escape.

What a woman did do was take an already existing male-invented staircase (or scaffolding) and move it outside of an already existing male-invented building in case of a fire.

If you look at any list of the top 100 inventions of all time and you will see some inventions that aren't that great always make the list because they were invented by women.

For example, baby food was invented by a woman, but

women didn't invent glass, the process of putting food in jars, and God created the ingredients.

Take a more recent female invention, Spanx. The material was not invented by a woman, the girdle was not invented by a woman, the factory that produced it was owned and operated by men. But the idea of a girdle that you put on and take off like shorts, that was invented by a woman.

What else? Kevlar, chocolate chip cookies... If you're interested in programming, there are two incremental improvements women had something to do with. Cobalt, the first compiler, and there was some algorithm... BUT The Microsoft commercial claims that the first computer algorithm was created by a woman, and it simply isn't true.

What you will not find on any list of female inventors are things like the automobile, assembly line manufacturing, guns, space ships, air planes, indoor plumbing, submarines, the film projector, air conditioning, farming equipment, the laboratory, alternate and direct current, the scientific method, the printing press, the telephone, the light bulb, anti-biotics, anesthesia, computers, the internet, etc.

This is by no means an exhaustive list, just a few monumental inventions that came from the top of our heads... Go on, try this at home.

Think of some significant advancement in the world, some invention that has become a part of your everyday life; so long as you're not thinking about chocolate chip cookies, then you'll be thanking a man... You're welcome.

11 – WOMEN CAN'T LEAVE OTHER COUNTRIES ALONE

Before women got the vote American men fiercely opposed America's involvement in foreign wars (especially in wars that involved crossing the Atlantic Ocean). George Washington had set this tradition in his final address as President.

When universal suffrage passed, political leaders then had a secure voting base that never really had to worry about *themselves* being drafted. Whereas there used to be periods of "peace time" now the United States is perpetually involved in conflicts overseas.

The basic idea here is, essentially, before women could vote, American men (who were the only voters) were very reluctant to vote for leaders who would take the country into war, especially foreign wars.

There were some minor military conflicts with Spain and Mexico, essentially little more than border conflicts. Then of course there was the civil war, which had nothing to do with external countries. WWI was the most notable foreign conflict prior to women voting but we will get to that in a bit.

One thing women have trouble doing is **leaving other countries alone**. The leaders are the result of female voters. At this point the main voting bloc is women. While there hasn't been a woman President, per se, we have been living under the "Women's Presidents" for almost a century. Since 1980 women have outvoted men in every presidential election but even before that they have been a sizable enough bloc to swing elections probably since Hoover.

It makes sense if you think about it; when men were voting, they also knew there was a draft. They knew that either themselves, or young men that were very much like themselves would be drawn into any foreign war. An escalated war could even lead to older men being drafted. Thus they were very hesitant to vote for war or vote for leaders who promoted war.

Remember, in World War I it took until the last year for America to get involved. Even then, it took the sinking of the Lusitania to get America to fight. Today, America is constantly at war; America is constantly involved in other country's affairs, whereas the male ethic is to live and let live (*especially when interfering could mean their gold or blood*).

There is a positive and negative aspect to the male ethic and it goes something like this: I got my stuff over here. I don't necessarily care about the people starving in another country, but I also don't want to blow their country up and kill people. I **definitely** don't want to do that if it means my taxes will go up or I might have to pay with my own life.

This might be somewhat counter-intuitive, going against the old cliché of men having something to prove, that warfare is an extension of man's testosterone-fueled-aggression guiding our foreign policy decisions.

First of all, testosterone is not a constant in a man's life. This much misunderstood hormone increases and decreases depending on what is being demanded from men at any given part of their life. Do they need to engage in battle or fierce competition? Then testosterone goes up (and up even higher when there is a win). Do they need to be calm and engage in methodical planning? Testosterone goes down.

For example, when a man is single and trying to find a woman his testosterone is pretty high. This is because he is in competition with other men for access to the eggs.

However, when a married man holds his first newborn baby in his hands studies have shown that his testosterone levels drop by a third almost instantly[12].

This is because the man has won the competition with other men. He was victorious and (the welfare state notwithstanding) this usually means he has already had to get resources to prove his worth in the first place to the woman.

So, from a biological perspective you have already figured out how to get a steady supply of resources, you have found a woman to mate with who (again without the welfare state and alimony) will be dependent on you to provide for her and the child while she is breastfeeding, etc. This should also mean that your access to her other eggs, in the future, is secured.

Biologically, now is the time to make calm, measured decisions so your testosterone goes down. Where bold risk-taking was required when you had neither resources nor access to eggs, now that same risk-taking could put at risk all that you have established in your life. So what does this all have to do with warfare?

Well, while it is true that men have access to Testosterone, which comes in handy when they are sent into

---

[12] The reason this happens upon holding your first child and not upon first having sex is that 1) not every woman can become pregnant and 2) not every pregnant woman is capable of successfully bearing the child to full term and through a successful birth. Remember, we are talking about biology not morality here.

battle, it is not true that it is some constant force that dominates their thinking in some uniform caricatured way throughout their life.

Testosterone (and the competitive aspect to the male makeup) is therefore a tool for males who have something to gain from some competitive battle. What do they have to gain from foreign conflicts? Why would men vote to get their country wrapped up in conflicts with countries they will never even visit? Even without the draft men naturally feel the pressure associated with stoking conflicts with other tribes. They know, deep down at a biological level, that if things get out of control, the draft will magically come back and if it really gets bad they could be drafting well into their 50's.

Remember, for thousands of years one tribe defeating another tribe usually meant **death** for the men and **new husbands** for the women.

While being taken as war booty (pun intended) may seem horrible, remember your genes only care that you pass on your genes and that there are resources to keep them alive. When your genes are still around long after you are dead they don't exactly care how they got there. Think about it, do you really care what your ancestors did 500 years ago to keep themselves alive? Does it materially affect your everyday life today?

Let's get back to women voters now that we have laid down the biological context. The women who have done most of the voting lately are not under all this pressure. Women essentially have nothing to lose from foreign wars. Since they don't have the subconscious fear of death that men have and like we covered in Chapter 3 women don't really pay taxes, you only need to present some semi-plausible reason to go to war and women generally will go for it[13].

---

[13] While there were conflicts before women started voting (which we are about to get into) don't discount women's role in militarizing men before they could vote. https://www.opendemocracy.net/5050/nicoletta-f-gullace/white-feather-girls-womens-militarism-in-uk

Also check out "The Origins of War in Child Abuse":

Remember when they first started to refer to "soccer moms" as a voting bloc? Soccer Moms were a way to group the female voters most easy to manipulate into a fear-state to justify war. See, there is a reason they chose soccer and not, say, baseball.

Soccer is one of those sports where you do not see individual achievement, for the most part. It is primarily group achievement. Therefore, there is almost no individual **failure** besides the goalie and the very rare auto-goal. The reason it is not Baseball Moms is because when you get up to the plate in baseball, you are going to fail most of the time. The parents have to have a little more of a steal stomach to weather the disappointment.

With Soccer Moms (who are so easily scared that they can't handle their kid failing at bat) any little thing can be used to manipulate them into being afraid of something in some other country.

Remember, the cost is nothing to them. They don't have that biological calculation for their personal well-being when there is a war. Remember, for thousands of years, tribal war really threatened the men more than the women. The women were loot. They're not as afraid as the men, who know that they could all be wiped out in a tribal conflict didn't go their way.

As a result, once women became a sizable voting bloc the leaders became much more willing to interfere in other countries' affairs. Foreign military engagements have gone through the roof but first let's look at this in terms of dollars and cents.

Military spending exploded, both in terms of real dollars spent and in terms of the percentage of GDP that is spent on "defense" spending. On the charts below I have marked with an X when women began to vote (in the US and in China).

https://www.youtube.com/watch?v=8oLl4oppAv4

Military Spending Explodes Shortly After Women First Get the Vote in America:

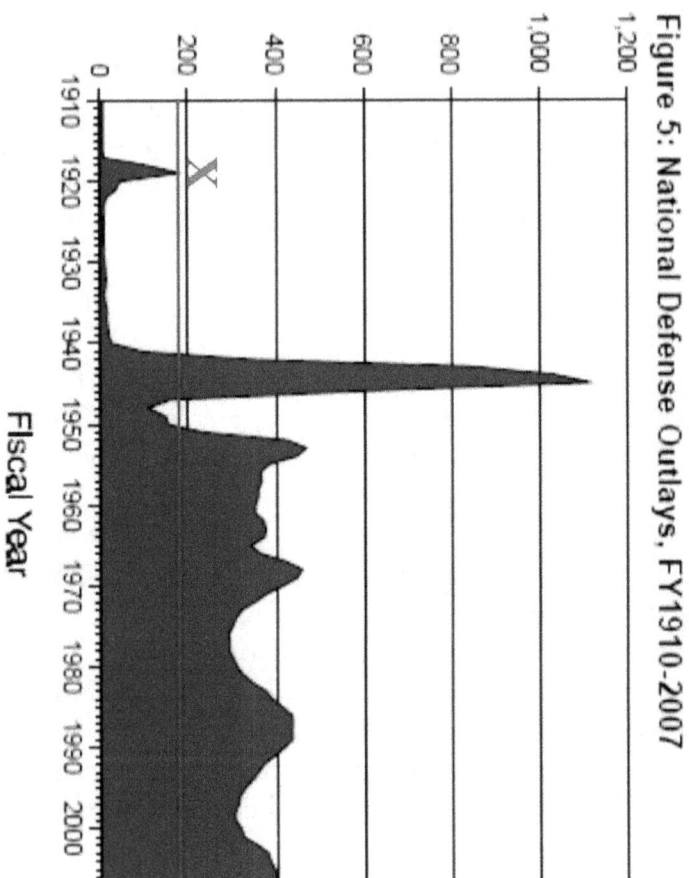

Figure 4 - Defense Spending in Real Dollars

Same thing happened in China when women began to be able to vote in 1949.

Of course, even more than in the United States it took a few election cycles for women to really get to the polls but the effect is the same, **extreme levels of militarization:**

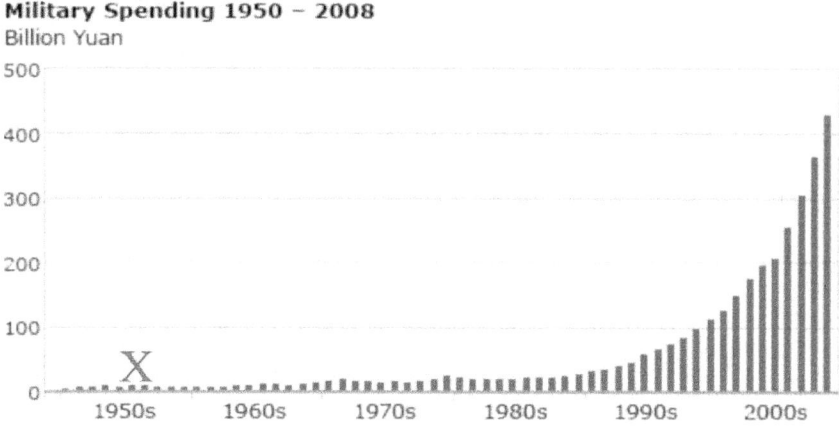

Figure 5 - Women Start Voting in 1949 China

This of course had a huge effect on the Federal Budget which hasn't been the same ever since women got the vote. Notice what happened to Federal spending once women got to pull the lever:

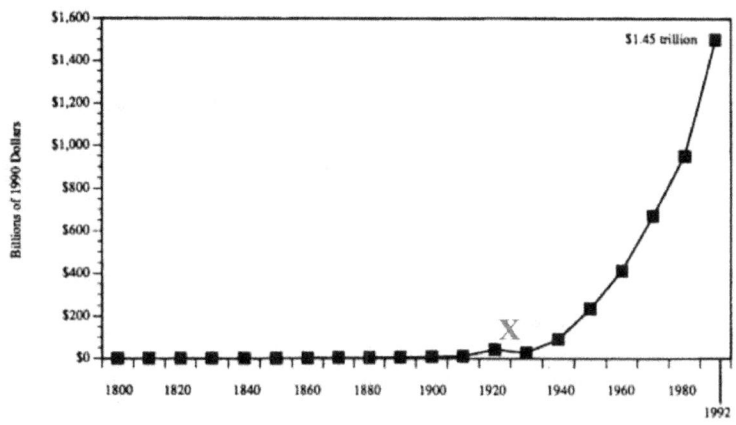

Pretty amazing! You can see when women starting voting the leaders knew that they could start spending like crazy.

Remember how the women didn't have the same biological reaction to foreign wars because their lives weren't on the line? Well the same goes for spending.

Women, as a group, weren't the ones having to pay the tax bill so any spending proposal sounds good if you aren't the one paying. To make the giant spending pill go down even easier politicians leaned more and more heavily on debt.

When most couples fight about money it is usually about the wife spending too much on the credit card. If you let them choose the leaders it shouldn't surprise you that our National Credit Card is getting maxed out.

Check out the following graphs which illustrate how much America's debt has exploded. Again, "X" marks the spot of when the ladies got to start voting (usually) for the tallest candidate.

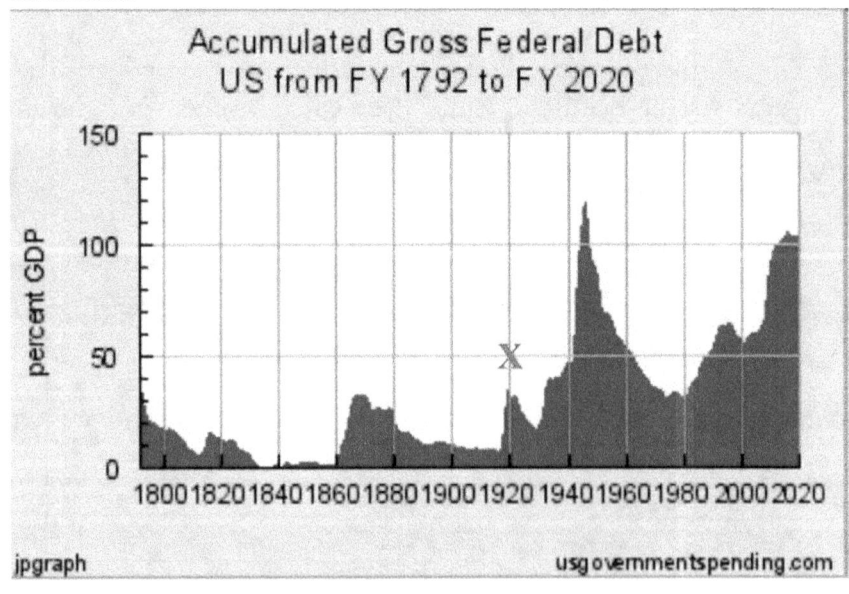

Figure 6 - Accumulated Debt as % GDP

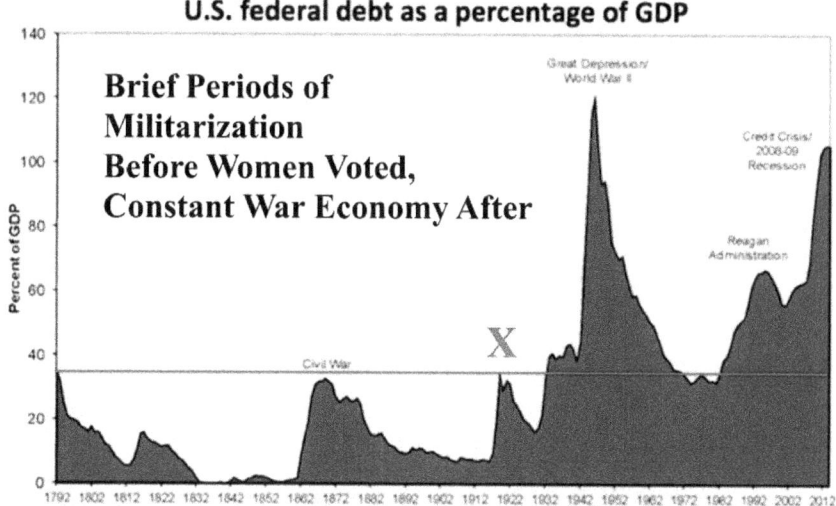

Figure 8 - War Time Debt Now Always Around

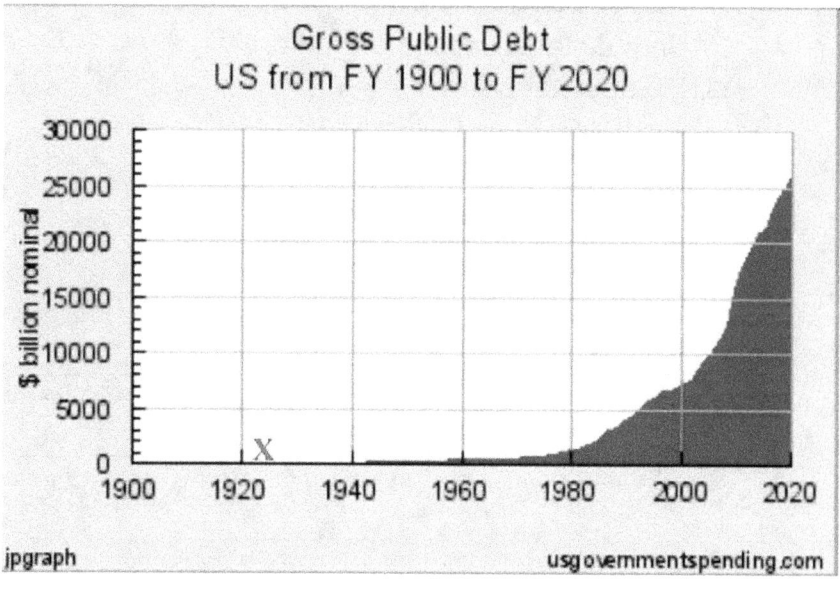

Figure 7 - Gross Public Debt

Getting back to women not being able to leave other countries alone, we need to take a look at the foreign conflicts America has had before women voted and after. First before women voted:

Foreign Conflicts Before Women Voted (1776 - 1924)

1) First Barbary War
2) 1811 German Coast Uprising
3) War of 1812
4) Second Barbary War
5) Great Lakes Basin (Canada?)
6) Mexican-American War
7) Filibuster War
8) Second Opium War
9) First and Second Cortina War
10) United States expedition to Korea
11) Rio de Janeiro Affair
12) Second Samoan Civil War
13) Spanish-American War
14) Philippine-American War
15) Boxer Rebellion
16) Occupation of Haiti
17) Banana Wars
18) WW1
19) Russian Civil War

As you can probably tell I am not cherry picking here. Even minor foreign conflicts are included here. Now at first blush the list of conflicts since women really started voting may not seem that much longer but consider a few things.

First, the list I'm about to show you covers a **period of just over 90 years**, whereas our previous list covers a period of about 150 years.

Second, while the previous list included a separate line for each foreign campaign; some on the next list represent **hundreds of micro-campaigns** in themselves. Without further ado here is the list of conflicts that occurred in just over 90 years of women voting:

Foreign Conflicts After Women Got the Vote
(1924 - 2016)

1) WW2
2) Korean War
3) Lebanon Crisis
4) Bay of Pigs Invasion
5) Simba Rebellion
6) Dominican Civil War
7) Vietnam War
8) Communist Insurgency in Thailand
9) Shaba II
10) Multinational Force in Lebanon
11) Invasion of Grenada
12) Tanker War
13) Invasion of Panama
14) Gulf War
15) Somali Civil War
16) Intervention in Haiti
17) Bosnian War
18) Kosovo War
19) War in Afghanistan
20) Iraq War

21) War in North-West Pakistan
22) 2011 Military Intervention in Libya
23) War on ISIL
24) War in Afghanistan (2015 - Present)
25) Pan Sahel Initiative (*this initiative alone got US involved in the military operations of Chad, Mali, Mauritania, Niger, Algeria, Morocco, Nigeria, Senegal, and Tunisia*)

Now like I said, some of these represent hundreds of military operations. This list also excludes completely covert operations that are responsible for assassinations and aiding foreign dictators (like Jimmy Carter's covert support for Pol Pot and the Khmer Rouge which killed millions).

In **2014 Alone** the US carried out **674 military missions across Africa**[14] which are all under the heading of the "Pan Sahel Initiative". Just remember that the next time someone says "if women had more power in the world it would be such a more peaceful place".

Yeah right! Women have been voting for a long time. They have essentially decided every election for decades so, yes, this is on them.

In fact, the political party most dominated by men today is the Libertarian party (almost 70% male). Is it any surprise that it is the only political party in America that advocates only using the military for purely self-defense related purposes?

War is not some "news event". Instead, war is men's money and men's lives on the line and deep down inside every man knows it.

---

[14] https://theintercept.com/2015/11/20/in-mali-and-rest-of-africa-the-u-s-military-fights-a-hidden-war/

12 – WOMEN CAN'T LEAVE INDIVIDUALS ALONE

America was different. No, really. It was. America "held truths to be self-evident". It was the "land of the free and the home of the brave." If somebody asked if they could sit[15] somewhere or speak their mind, "it's a free country" was a common response; when people said it, it was without irony.

There were laws, sure; there were even some taxes, though very little. You could say what you wanted, write what you wanted. You could sell what you wanted, wherever you wanted. You could buy what you wanted, drink what you wanted. What you did to your own property, on your own property (short of murder, kidnapping, rape, assault and robbery) was between you, God and your family.

Throughout history, the societies that thrived the most were those that governed the least. America was no exception. Liberty and freedom, besides being kind of nice, helped build America into the economic superpower of the world. We were a city on a hill, the exception, set apart from the harsh strictures of tyrants, oligarchs and dictators.

Today there are millions of laws, rules and regulations that tightly rule our daily lives. In January of 2012, 40,000 state laws took effect controlling everything from getting jobs in Alabama, education about gays and lesbians in California and golf cart safety in Georgia. At the same time the federal government passed a law fining truckers and bus drivers $2,700 every time they used their cell phone while driving.

There is no possible way that any of us could ever read all of the laws that apply to us. Most of us just try to live our

---

[15] Rosa Parks notwithstanding.

lives and do the "right" thing, but that is no guarantee that men with guns won't show up at your door enforcing some obscure regulation you didn't even know existed. Often these regulations carry more than just a stiff fine.

An Alaskan inventor who never had so much as a traffic ticket was arrested, indicted and prosecuted by the federal government because he failed to put the right sticker on a UPS package. He had no idea the sticker was required, and everything else about his shipment was perfectly legal. After being arrested and handcuffed by a half-dozen SWAT-team officers aiming assault rifles at him, his face down on the pavement, he spent almost two years in a federal prison.

Fisherman David McNab, a seafood distributor and importer, is serving an eight-year sentences in three U.S. prisons because he packed his catch in a manner that (allegedly) violated Honduran regulation. The highest officials of the Honduran government certified that McNab had, in fact, violated no Honduran law, but that made no difference to the American courts.

Recently federal legislation suggests that anyone who violates the rules of an online social networking site, such as MySpace or Facebook, by registering with a false name could spend up to five years in federal prison.

The problem is SO pervasive that most people don't even notice. Like the frog in boiling water, the country changed over time. Younger people never knew any different.

Below is a list of some of commonplace examples of how American freedom is an oxymoron. As you look them over, ask yourself, "Is this America? Is this freedom? Is this what the founding fathers fought for? What type of human being would make these rules?"

#1 In Hazelwood, Missouri it is illegal for little girls to sell girl scout cookies in the front yards of their own homes.

#2 All over the United States lemonade stands run by children are being shut down because they do not have the proper permits.

#3 San Francisco has implemented a ban on Happy Meal toys.

#4 In Minnetonka, Minnesota you can be fined up to $2,000 for having a muddy vehicle.

#5 It is illegal to give a tour of the monuments in Washington D.C. without a license.

#6 In many U.S. states it is now illegal to collect any rain that falls on your own property.

#7 In San Juan Capistrano, California it is against the law to hold a home Bible study without a "conditional use permit".

#8 In America today it is illegal to milk your cow and sell the milk to your neighbor. If you do this, there is a good chance that federal agents will raid your home at the crack of dawn. (While we're on the subject of milk, it is illegal to deface a milk carton in the state of Massachusetts.)

#9 The following are just some of the cities that use RFID tracking chips to monitor the recycling habits of their citizens:

* Cleveland, Ohio
* Charlotte, North Carolina
* Alexandria, Virginia
* Boise, Idaho
* Dayton, Ohio
* Flint, Michigan

#10 It is illegal to operate a train in the United States that does not have an "F" painted on the front. Apparently without that "F" we all might not know where the front of the train is.

What happened? What happened to the "land of the free" and "don't tread on me?" The short answer to the question is... WOMEN. Women happened.

I know it may seem unfair to blame women for this intrusion on personal liberties, but consider the following:

- The chronology of the nanny state directly corresponds with women's suffrage.
- Women are now the majority of America's voting pool.

What was the first political agenda that motivated women, even before the right to vote? Prohibition. Forcing the state to get their husbands to stop drinking.

Prohibition led to mass murder, corruption and mayhem as well as the proliferation of organized crime. When that failed and was overturned, they moved on to the (unconstitutional[16]) war on drugs; today there are more black prisoners in America than there were American slaves, in large part due to this feminized nanny-state drug war.

But don't try to make this point on your blog or twitter feed. It is now practically illegal to offend people on the internet.

---

[16] We say unconstitutional because, HELLO, they needed an amendment to get the Federal government into the prohibition game for alcohol. That amendment has been repealed and no corresponding amendment was ever ratified for the prohibition of other substances.

13 – WOMEN CAN'T WORK OVERTIME

As perfectly explained in the chapter *"Women Cant Deserve 100 Cents on the Dollar"* there are plenty of good reasons women don't earn as much as men (as a whole). There is, however, something we didn't really get into in that chapter.

Something so simple that women could fix (if they were so inclined); something that would drastically narrow the so-called "wage gap". That is the **gender-hours gap**, which (along with taking dangerous jobs) is a close cousin of the gender-wage gap. **Work more, earn more**... *not exactly rocket science ladies.*

Most people have heard that full-time working women in America earn only 83 cents for every dollar earned by men (*oh, the poor put upon women!*)

This is true only in the most **misleading** sense. These numbers don't take into account the number of hours actually worked. As it turns out, women work fewer hours than men (BIG surprise).

The Labor Department defines full-time as 35 hours[17] a week or more, and the "or more" is far more likely to refer to male workers than to female ones.

According to the department, almost 55% of workers logging more than 35 hours a week are men. If you defined full time as 40 hours or more the percentage would be much higher for men.

In 2007, 25% of men working full-time jobs had workweeks exceeding 40 hours (of 41 or more hours), compared with just 14% of female full-time workers. In other words, the infamous gender-wage gap is to a large degree just a **gender-hours gap**.

---

[17] What are we, France?

This is the part where all the excuses and accusations come. *It's all men's fault because they don't want to stay home and rear the kids while the women work overtime.*

Well, for those of you that A) see this hour's gap/wage gap as a problem (I certainly don't) and B) want to follow the feminist tradition of blaming all your problems on men, I have this to say:

TAKE IT UP WITH NATURE!

There is simply no way for men to fill in during the pregnancy months. To keep it really simple so even feminists understand:

1. Men do not have the organs required for gestation.
2. They also do not have mammary glands that allow women to lactate and feed weening children.

So that is essentially 3 years of downtime that needs to happen for women, per child. If the population is going to remain stable women need to have 2.2 kids each, 3 each if there is going to be growth. So that is like 9 years of downtime.

But can't the mom pump and shouldn't companies just make it so super easy to work while you are pregnant, etc, etc?

NO, just no. I'm trying to keep this simple so even the over-fed feminists can follow. Work = Stress; Stress = bad for pregnancy; therefore, Work = bad for pregnancy.

As mentioned, it is extremely important that the mother breastfeed for the first 18 months. Forgoing breastfeeding can lower the child's IQ by at least 5 points, not to mention the other related health problems.

As far as **pumping, it is just NOT the same thing**. Breast milk is meant to be taken directly. In this way if the child is more thirsty than hungry they can just drink for a short session. If the child is really hungry then they can continue to feed and the initial thin/watery milk is slowly replaced by thicker milk that nourishes as a meal.

Pumping does not allow for this mechanism to function. You end up training your child that every time they are thirsty they should eat rather than drink. It should be obvious that this can lead to obesity later in life.

Now as far as companies taking a "kinder and gentler approach to family life events", just grow up. It's funny how women did not give two thoughts about parental leave until they started to take a larger share in the workplace. It is this attitude itself that causes women to earn less.

That isn't a problem in itself. **I for one celebrate individual woman's choices** to avoid dangerous jobs, avoid overtime and choose enjoyable professions (over income maximizing career choices).

I just don't appreciate men being demonized as dissertating women in the workplace just because they rightfully earn less.

As a society we should really ask ourselves what **our obsession is with sex parity**. We are biologically so different. What is wrong with men and women specializing in different areas of life with, of course, a significant amount of overlap?

14 – WOMEN CAN'T TEACH CHILDREN TO SPEAK

You would think with most women not working overtime, with many working part-time or not at all that they would be the ones imparting language skills to their children. WRONG! The fact is that nothing could be further from the truth. Virtually all home-based advanced language skills are passed on from Father to child (otherwise not passed on at all).

There is virtually no difference in language development between children raised with or without their mothers. On the other hand, the absence of the father drastically reduces advanced language development.

This is obvious to anyone that has spent any considerable time within America's inner cities. America's cities are plagued with almost exclusively single-mother led households. These children of single mothers have almost zero verbal skills. You can hardly understand what they are saying and, when you can understand, it is clear that grammar, sentence structure, diction, and content are all a mess.

If these children had never met their mothers and had been raised solely in daycare the children could hardly be less communicative.

Notice the following from Today.com, taken from the article "How fathers boost toddlers' language development":

> *Fathers "made unique contributions to children's expressive language development" that went "above and beyond" the contributions of education and child care.*

> *When fathers used more words with their children during play, children had more advanced language skills a year later. The implication is that fathers may also be making important contributions to their children's later success in school.*

This was based on research of middle class families. They mention in the article that the researchers tried to see if this somehow changed in poorer families but found pretty much the same result with children from neighborhoods where half the families were below the poverty line:

> *A total of 1,292 infants in two parent families participated in the study. The researchers visited the children's families when the children were six months old, fifteen months old, and three years old.*

> *They found that fathers' education and their use of vocabulary when reading picture books to their*

children at six months of age were significantly related to the children's expressiveness at fifteen months and use of advanced language at age three. This held true **no matter what the mother's educational level was or how she spoke** *to the children. (emphasis ours)*

Lack of verbal skills significantly increases the chance that the child will eventually be incarcerated. Notice the following taken from "The relationship between lower intelligence, crime and custodial outcomes":

Preliminary research has proposed that IQ differences between offender and non-offender populations may be attributed to verbal reasoning (Blackburn, 1999)[18].

So if you want your child to be able to speak and have the best chance of avoiding "the clink" then you probably will need their fathers to stick around. *Oh no, generalizations! NAWALT! BUT...* I refer all you nitpickers to chapter one explaining why most women (and beta-males) are incapable of understanding this book.

---

[18] This is in reference to the following study: Blackburn, R. (1999). The psychology of criminal conduct: Theory research and practice (4th ed.). New York: Wiley & Sons.

15 – WOMEN CAN'T HAVE IT ALL *(Be Great Mothers AND Great Employees)*

The basic idea here is that the concept of a "working mom" is essentially a myth.

We're going to sum up a really good video Stefan Molyneux did when he was guest hosting Peter Schiff's show. He titled the video, "The Mythology of the Working Mom" (the following quotes are paraphrased for brevity).

In it he explains that working mothers are not really a thing. Either you are a mom, or you are working full time. Or you are doing part of one and part of the other, but you can't really do both of those things well.

A female caller calls up, all upset because she works really hard and she claims that her kids do not suffer. Then he starts to break it down. He says, "Okay, so you're saying that you work just as hard as a man?" She responds, "oh yeah. Absolutely."

He asks, "Okay, so do your kids need to be picked up from school?"

She responds, "Well, yeah, I leave right at five because they do after school activities."

"Ok, so, after school activities. They're not spending any time with you. And you leave right at 5 O'clock, so that means you can't really be there for work, right? Because the guys will stay till 6/7/8 or 9 if they have to for something."

She then explains, "Yeah, but then I get back on my laptop at home and I'll do work then."

Molyneux then tries to figure out if she is a good worker or a good mother, because you really can't be both. He starts running through all of the time she is spending at work. It basically came down to that she was more or less a good worker, and not a good mom.

56 hours sleep, 60 work, 10 commuting, 20 hours "me" time, 6 hours gym, plenty left for the kids...

She explained that her kids have all of these activities they go to. She and her husband both work so the kids can do Jujitsu and other activities that cost money.

Molyneux explains that time spent doing those activities is time spent with people who are not their parents. It worked out where she had about an hour a day with the kids. That hour was the worst hour of the day when she had to make dinner after being exhausted from a day of work and errands. She then said, "well, I get these vacations."

"Okay, so that's like one or two weeks out of the year that you actually get to mother your children, or give your children get proper attention. That's dreadful, but very common."

They really can't have it all. Now, to some extent men could be the ones staying home giving primary care to kids while the women work.

But then you still have the problem of downtime inherent with a woman's pregnancy and subsequent breastfeeding. Pumping before work is NOT the same thing.

As mentioned in Chapter 13 (*and purposefully repeated here because of its importance*), sometimes when the infant is breastfeeding it is just thirsty and sometimes it is hungry. The human female breasts are designed to first give very watery "milk" (that is like taking a drink of water) and then if the child continues to feed it will switch to thicker milk (that is more of a meal). Pumping means your child will always be fed meal-thick milk even when they are just thirsty. Hmmm, I wonder if a pattern of eating when you are just thirsty will have negative effects as an adult?

Also having stress while you are pregnant. They have established that stress during pregnancy does all kinds of bad things for the kid. If your cortisol levels are going up while you are pregnant, that increases your likelihood of complications with the pregnancy and birth.

If you are a good mother, you are going to try to take it easy while you're pregnant. You are going to breastfeed for at least 18 months, because IQ correlates with breast feeding. There are at least 5 IQ points that depend on being breast fed.

There is thus a necessity to have about 2 to 3 years of downtime for each kid. If we are going to continue to have a human race, we need to have 2 to 3 kids per family just to continue steady population. Therefor this idea that woman can pursue a stressful full-time careers, have 2 to 3 kids, raise them with the proper nourishment and care they need, model a healthy marital relationship with their Husbands AND be truly happy with life is just absurd.

There's this episode of Oprah where she has a woman crying on the show. The working mother explains that she wakes up at dawn just to make cookies for her kids, because she associates cookie making with motherhood. As in, "*Yeah, I work these long hours, but at least my child eats cookies.*"

In the meantime, she is crying on national television because of the basic fact that she can't do both very well simultaneously. And yet we are bombarded with this image over and over again in sitcom and TV drama over and over again.

Two parents are working. They appear to have it all, even if they sometimes seemed over-worked and tired. Nobody is allowed to make the point that this is not for the benefit of the children you are raising.

During the heyday of Murphy Brown, Vice-President Dan Quayle said one off-handed comment that it doesn't help to have fictional characters like Murphy Brown glorifying working single-motherhood. He made the point that this might not be the best role-model for young people.

This caused a huge controversy and media battle between the Republican Vice-President and the creators of Murphy Brown. Since people were entertained by Murphy Brown, she naturally got more sympathizers. Years later Candice Bergen, the **actress playing Murphy Brown, admitted that Dan Quayle was right**.

Even if he was wrong, the fact that he couldn't even voice this as a concern should be disconcerting. The truth is that while Murphy Brown is a fictional character, most people watching the show would not have her job or luxurious life-style and income. Even on this fictitious show, she has a painter friend of hers helping to raise her child.

More recently a woman, who was working for Hillary Clinton, wrote an article and was interviewed on NPR, basically saying that she tried to have it all, and couldn't. She had this dream job, working for the Secretary of State that she thought she wanted, but the truth is that it did not make her happy. She felt like she couldn't really talk to anybody about it because she was supposed to be happy. Society, from the moment she was a child, told her that this lifestyle was supposed to bring her happiness. There was nothing wrong about her job, it's prestige or her pay. Ultimately she missed seeing her husband, she missed seeing her kids. Ultimately, she resigned. However, in every interview she had, she went out of her way to make the point that this preference does not apply to everybody. "This is just me". She almost seemed to be afraid of being attacked for stating and living a preference for the benefit of her children, herself and, while we're at it, her husband.

That is the nature of **political correctness** (which is often the opposite of **actual correctness**). Ignoring or downplaying your own **lived experience**. She was talking about her own lived experience, but had to preface with a whole bunch of caveats. Another interesting thing is that she never felt this way when she worked for universities, because those are somewhat fake jobs.

Working for the State department is kind of also a fake job, because it is government stuff, but it IS hard. If you are at the high levels of government, as she was, it is hard. You have to actually put in the hours if you are an undersecretary reporting to Hillary Clinton. That is a serious job. These jobs at universities, which are all kind of made up jobs from the government, a lot of these people are putting in 16 hour weeks. So, sure, a person can work 16 hours a week and still be a mom, when you have the university providing all the day care for your brief periods of work.

DAYCARE KILLS

We are having a lot of fun writing this book but let's get serious for a moment about something that is NOT funny: SIDS. The full name is the ambiguous "Sudden Infant Death Syndrome".

Sounds fancy but SIDS is a little-understood phenomenon where the child just suddenly dies (as the name suggests). While it is not fully understood what is causing these sudden deaths what is clear is the correlation between SIDS and Daycare. If you combine SIDS deaths at Day Care Facilities with SIDS deaths at "family" day care (read: not your family) then **day care** accounts for a **whopping 80% of SIDS deaths**.

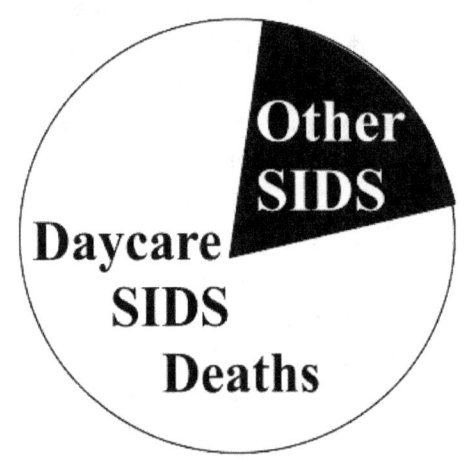

There is just no substitute for the actual parents raising the children.

RECOMMENDED VIEWING:
The Mythology of the Working Mom:
https://www.youtube.com/watch?v=ORCOn97I2ko

RECOMMENDED READING:
Daycare and SIDS:
http://www.firstcandle.org/sids-and-daycare-a-fatal-combination/

Dan Quayle Was Right:
http://www.people.com/people/article/0,,624379,00.html
https://www.washingtonpost.com/opinions/20-years-later-it-turns-out-dan-quayle-was-right-about-murphy-brown-and-unmarried-moms/2012/05/25/gJQAsNCJqU_story.html

16 – WOMEN CAN'T DIRECT MOVIES

What's your favorite movie of all time? It's hard, right? To pick one movie out of ALL the movies that have been made over the past hundred and ten years, and say "this one is my favorite". For a movie to even come to mind as a favorite movie contender, it has to be pretty special, pretty remarkable.

It had to touch you, move you in some profound way. If you're like me, you've seen it countless times, recommend it to friends, family, people you're dating. You can quote from it; you can close your eyes and conjure up scenes from it.

Well, what comes to mind? It doesn't have to be just one; think of a few. Which movie can you just watch and re-watch over and over? No matter how many times you've seen it, you always catch something new.

Maybe you like gangster films, movies that deal with an alternative moral compass, unexpected violence and the dark underbelly of the American Dream: The Godfather, Goodfellas, Pulp Fiction, Scarface or Donnie Brasco?

Maybe you really like fantasy, that type of imaginary escapism of an alternate world: The Lord of the Rings (any of the 3), Harry Potter (any of the 7), Pirates of the Caribbean (any of the 3) or Pan's Labrynth

Maybe you're into Science Fiction because you like your fantasy escapism to take place on other planets or in the future: Star Wars (tho technically this takes places in the past, not the future), 2001: A Space Odyssey, Terminator 2, 12 Monkeys, Blade Runner, The Matrix.

Maybe you love to laugh, so your favorite movie (if you really think about it, and if we're really being honest with ourselves) is a comedy that doesn't take itself too seriously:

History of the World Part 1, Network, Airplane, Elf, Annie Hall, My Blue Heaven, The Princess Bride, Duck Soup, Three Amigos, The Big Lebowski, There's Something About Mary, Knocked Up, Monty Python and the Holy Grail.

You like war movies? Blood, guts, bullets, Jerries and glory? Apocolypse Now, Full Metal Jacket, Saving Private Ryan, Platoon, The Deer Hunter, Three Kings, Jarhead, Inglorious Bastards.

One completely American genre is that of the Western, with its vast landscapes, depictions of a simpler bygone era, and the no-man's land of law and order? Unforgiven, The Good, The Bad and The Ugly, Rio Bravo, Django Unchained, Tombstone, High Noon, The Searchers and Stage Coach

Superhero movies? Any Batman, any Spiderman, any Iron Man, either Avengers or either Hellboy make your top lists?

Are you a child at heart? Maybe you take every vacation at Disney Land / World because of how much you love those movies: Little Mermaid, Lion King, Snow White or Peter Pan. More recently there have been some really great 3D animated children's movies, especially from Pixar: Toy Story, The Incredibles, Monsters Inc. and Finding Nemo always seem to make people's top lists, even adults.

Are you a child of the 80s? Nothing wrong with a little Goonies, Ferris Beuhler, Breakfast Club, Amadeus, Indiana Jones, Roger Rabbit, E.T. Tootsie and Beetlejuice.

Maybe you're into really old movies from the golden age of the studio system: Citizen Kane, The Treasure of Sierra Madre, Gone With The Wind, On The Waterfront, Rebel Without a Cause, Some Like It Hot and Casablanca.

Scary Movies? What's your favorite scary movie? Scream, Halloween (remake or original), The Shining, The Exorcist, Psycho, The Ring, Evil Dead, Hostel, Saw, Hellraiser, Friday the 13th, Psycho, Nightmare on Elm Street, Paranormal Activity, The Witch...

Too dark? Maybe you like a little song and dance in your movies. There's just something about the whimsical nature of your favorite musical that always cheers you up: West Side Story, My Fair Lady, The Sound of Music, The Wizard of Oz, Singin' In The Rain, Chicago, Les Miserables, Cabaret, Hair, The Rocky Horror Picture Show, Chicago.

Now, this is by no means a comprehensive list of every great movie ever made, but you have to admit, it's a pretty diverse group of classic films from different time periods in different genres. There's gotta be some movies on that list that you absolutely LOVE, couldn't imagine living without. I'd venture to say that if you knew somebody who had never seen a single movie - an Amish person, an Aboriginea... a cave man thawed from a block of ice or an alien from another planet -- you could do far worse than the above titles to give them an idea of why movies are so magical, what movies ARE and what they CAN BE.

Other than their fame, greatness, timelessness and commercial success... you know one thing ALL these films have in common? Every one of them? They were ALL directed by MEN.

Of course, I haven't covered every great movie in existence, but that's not really the point. While there ARE female directors and some very good movies were directed by women... even some great ones, chances are... if you're being honest with yourself, your favorite movie was not directed by a woman.

Try it out on someone nearby; ask the nearest person (or even a feminist) what his or her favorite movie is, then look up who directed it. In fact, unless your favorite movie is on the list below, I would say it is VERY unlikely it had a female director.

Catherine Hardwicke - Thirteen, Lords of Dogtown, Twilight
Betty Thomas - Private Parts, The Brady Bunch Movie
Penny Marshall - Big, A League of Their Own
Kimberly Pierce - Boys Don't Cry, Stop Loss
Kathryn Bigelow - Point Break, The Hurt Locker, Zero Dark Thirty
Sofia Coppola - Lost In Translation, Virgin Suicides, Marie Antoinette
Julie Taymor - Frida,
Nora Ephron - Sleepless in Seattle, You've Got Mail, Julie and Julia
Barbara Kopple - Harlan County, U.S.A., Shut Up & Sing
Jane Campion - The Piano, Sweetie
Debra Granik - Winter's Bone, Down To The Bone
Miranda July - Me, You and Everyone We Know
Sharon Maguire - Bridget Jones's Diary, Bridget Jones's Baby
Tamra Davis - Half Baked, Billy Madison
Vicky Jensen - Shrek (which she CODIRECTED with a MAN)
Jennifer Lee - Frozen (which she CODIRECTED with a MAN)
Ann Fletcher - Step Up, 27 Dresses, The Proposal
Phyllida Lloyd - Mamma Mia, The Iron Lady
Penelope Spheeris - Wayne's World, The Little Rascals, Black Sheep

Mimi Leder - Deep Impact, Pay It Forward
Barbra Streisand - The Prince of Tides, Yentl
Amy Heckerling - Clueless, Fast Times at Ridgemont High, Look Who's Talking, Johnny Dangerously
Nancy Meyers - The Holiday, Something's Gotta Give, The Parent Trap, The Intern

My personal favorite movies on the above list are probably the comedies: Wayne's World, Half Baked and Private Parts. If there were some elaborate reason why I could never see those movies ever again, could never show them to my children or loved ones, I would be pretty sad... but I would get over it. It's hard to say the same for EVERY OTHER MOVIE EVER MADE.

But maybe this is a bad way to make this point. After all, who am I to decide what qualifies as a great movie? With all due respect, who are you? Maybe a better way would be to look at the Academy Awards. I mean, they're a well-respected, revered (liberal) organization? What do they think of female directors?

METACRITIC PUT IT THIS WAY:

> *"When Kathryn Bigelow collected her Oscar trophy earlier this year, she did so as only the fourth woman ever nominated in the director category. But the Academy certainly isn't the only organization to OVERLOOK female directors; Bigelow is also the only female to win BAFTA and DGA awards as top director, and Barbra Streisand is the only female Golden Globe-winning director."* (emphasis added)

In the HISTORY of the Academy Awards, only one woman has won best director. Metacritic attributes this anomaly to female directors being overlooked, as if female directors have been making the best movies for years, but have just been unfairly ignored by every major awards organization.

It's possible. Remember too that many movies go unappreciated in their time. It often takes years, even decades for the greatness, influence and significance of any work of art to be understood and appreciated. Van Gogh never sold one painting. It wasn't until the 50s that Citizen Kane was appreciated. Same goes for the 90s and Raging Bull. So, what about an organization that is meant to appreciate films that have been out for decades, sometime more than a century?

The original goal of the American Film Institute was to restore and protect great movies from the wear and tear of deterioration. As a way to raise money for their organization they started ti poll filmmakers and movie critics to make lists of the greatest American Films of all time.

For the first 100 years of cinema, they put together a list called 100 years 100 movies. Not a single movie was directed by a woman. The British Film Institute does the same thing with a top 10 list every 10 years. They've never featured a movie directed by a woman.

But those lists were put together by film critics and film directors, two professions dominated by males. Maybe box office returns are the best way to judge women's contribution to the film industry; it's certainly the most democratic and the least susceptible to chauvinism. Does anybody believe that audiences go to the movies to subjugate women?

Highest-grossing films adjusted for inflation as of 2014

Rank	Title	Worldwide gross (2014 $)	Year
1	_Gone with the Wind_	$3,440,000,000	1939
2	_Avatar_	$3,020,000,000	2009
3	_Star Wars_	$2,825,000,000	1977
4	_Titanic_	ᵀ$2,516,000,000	1997
5	_The Sound of Music_	$2,366,000,000	1965
6	_E.T. the Extra-Terrestrial_	$2,310,000,000	1982
7	_The Ten Commandments_	$2,187,000,000	1956
8	_Doctor Zhivago_	$2,073,000,000	1965
9	_Jaws_	$2,027,000,000	1975
10	_Snow White and the Seven Dwarfs_	ˢ$1,819,000,000	1937

That's just the top 10. You can go through the top 100 grossing movies (link below), and not find one movie directed by a woman. http://www.filmsite.org/boxoffice3.html

[For a moment I thought number 97 on the list, The Hunger Games: Catching Fire had a female director, but it turns out Francis Lawrence is a man's name.]

Or maybe the highest grossing movies go mainly to super hero movies and action films, two genres that favor the male gender. What about so called chick flicks? Movies about relationships, weddings, Hugh Grant, feelings and romance?

The Notebook, When Harry Met Sally, Love Actually, Grease, Notting Hill, 4 Weddings and a Funeral, Breakfast at Tiffany's, Dirty Dancing, Bridesmaids, Titanic, The First Wive's Club, Gone With The Wind, My Best Friend's Wedding, The Apartment, Casablanca, 10 Things I Hate About You, Legally Blonde, Moulin Rouge, Miss Congeniality, SEX AND THE CITY (!)... even a movie called How To Lose a Guy In 10 Days.

You know how guys are always portrayed as brash and insensitive, callous to the evolved, yet complicated emotions of the opposite sex? LOOK AT THAT LIST OF CHICK FLICKS! Every one of them was directed by a man. (To be fair, while men are often portrayed in movies as brash and insensitive, chances are those scenes were directed BY men, so we only have ourselves to blame.)

Okay. So like, what's up? -But REALLY though. I mean, by every kind of measurement you can think of, with every qualifier imaginable, women cannot direct movies. Why not?

To be completely and perfectly honest with you, I DON'T KNOW. It's not like women have done something wrong by NOT being film directors. People are different from each other, with different strengths, different weaknesses, different views, different ways we interact with people and the world around us. Being honest about those differences is one of the most challenging and rewarding aspects of the human experience. It's the implicit goal of psychologists, anthropologists and artists the world over.

And yet, when this phenomenon DOES get addressed by Social Justice Warriors, the reason for this disparity is blamed on 2 things.

1. Women HAVE been directing great movies. Their efforts go ignored and unappreciated by a male

dominated dictatorship, or

2. Women haven't been given enough opportunities to make great movies... by a male dominated dictatorship.

Take the Metacritic article referenced earlier:

> *"The Cannes Film Festival also has a POOR RECORD in RECOGNIZING the ACHIEVEMENTS of women directors, and this year the festival came under fire when not a single one of the 18 films selected for the main competition were directed by women." (emphasis added)*

The Cannes Film Festival has a poor record of recognizing the achievements of women directors? The writer of the article does not even allow for the possibility that WOMEN DIRECTORS have a POOR RECORD of directing films WORTH recognizing.

Metacritic goes on to say:

> *"... Not every genre has been open to directors of all genders; for example, few women other than Bigelow or Mimi Leder (Deep Impact) have ever had the opportunity to direct an action film."*

It's like there's this vast genital conspiracy perpetrated by an ol' boy network of financiers, studio heads and movie producers who secretly organize to keep women down. Male domination then begets male domination, and lo and behold it is the fault of a powerful male patriarchy that women are not making greater movies more often.

It just... It just doesn't work that way. Not everybody can perform exactly the same. How hard would it be for every single profession to be represented completely equally by race, gender, politics and creed? Equality does not equal sameness. That doesn't mean somebody is being discriminated against.

You can have a quota at a police department and force a bunch of women to become police officers, but when you are making about female police officers (The Heat), there are millions of dollars at stake; it has to perform financially. Generally speaking, financiers don't care HOW they make their money back. They just want to make money, and it is very hard to shield a multi-million-dollar private investment from, ya know... numbers and reality.

And what's all this about certain genres not being "open to female directors", or a "lack of opportunities" for the fairer sex? Everything is as open to people as it could possibly be, especially nowadays. Between digital cameras (invented by men), non-linear editing software (do I even have to say it?) and LED lighting, it has never been cheaper to shoot your magnum opus.

What could possibly have prevented women from making the micro-budget Paranormal Activity, Open Water or The Blair Witch Project? Whatever the answer, sexist studio heads did not play a part.

Also, female directors aren't getting opportunities from whom? From studio heads? Well, who built studios like Warner Brothers, MGM and Disney? Those studios were built by men. They didn't have lots of "opportunities". They made their own. Why didn't women build any movie studios? Lots of women had money at the turn of the 20th century (the suffrage movement would not have happened without wealthy women). Not one of them had the ability or inclination to start a movie studio. If they had, they could have distributed as many opportunities to as many female directors as they wanted...

Was it a lack of role models? Lack of encouragement? Negative articles like this one took the wind out of the sails of potential female auteurs? Maybe if I could just shut up, Stephanie Kubrick and Wilma Disney would dazzle the silver screens...

But role models and encouragement were not the reasons great film makers and studio heads made movies. Nobody encouraged the Warner family to sell their golden watch heirloom and invest their horse carriage income to start a movie studio. What "role models" did they have to "encourage" them to learn film photography and development (invented by men), visual storytelling, finance, and distribution?

Later on the Warner brothers bet the farm on talkies, incorporating recorded sound to their feature length films. They had a success with Al Jolson in the famous Jazz Singer (now considered one of the greatest movies of all time), but it could have just as easily bankrupted the studio. They were trailblazers, with no male role models to look up to or emulate and no opportunity given to them because of their gender.

These men should be admired for their vision, respected for their bravery. Instead, studios and producers are labeled sexist for not sharing opportunities equally among the genders. It's not fair. More importantly, IT DOESN'T HELP. Crying sexism every time things don't go your way doesn't solve anything... unless you're Gretchen Carlson.

17 – WOMEN CAN'T NOT RUIN GHOSTBUSTERS

Ghostbusters may have been the most controversial movie of 2016, causing many a blogosphere and twitterverse to go berserk. The official trailer for the Ghostbusters remake was the lowest rated YouTube trailer ever, garnering over a million thumbs downs. Leaving negative comments on the YouTube trailer became a sort of internet meme in and of itself (sort of the opposite of the 3 Wolves t-shirt reviews on Amazon), until YouTube deactivated the comments section (because, you know, opinions are dangerous).

This prompted a never ending onslaught of YouTube rant videos, blog posts and retweets. Fans of the original flooded IMDB to bring down the remake's rating before the movie was even released. The backlash against the movie created its own backlash when two of the film's stars became defensive about the criticism (more on that later).

Breitbart's tech editor Milo Yiannopoulos was suspended from Twitter for his views on the film and its stars; he was then reinstated after a backlash to the backlash to the original backlash. In effect, Ghostbusters had broken the Internet (and without nudity *thank goodness*).

So, what was all the hubbub and hullabaloo about anyways? Well, the long awaited Ghostbusters reboot replaced the crew with all female actors. Not a big deal, you say? Grow up? It's just a movie? Get over it? Okay, fair enough I suppose. But then again, let me ask you something. Have you ever LOVED anything before?

If you love something, you love it for what it IS or you don't love it at all. A museum might restore a Picasso, but they wouldn't rearrange the eyes to make them even. You wouldn't level the Leaning Tower of Piza, gild a lily or put Fat Albert on a diet. So, why are you castrating the Ghostbusters?

I Ain't Afraid Of No Hoes.

I'm not positive what a **cause célèbre** is exactly, but I'm pretty sure this qualifies.

How you feel about this franchise reboot probably says more about you than your favorite band or political party affiliation.

Try to understand this from a guy's perspective. The preview showed a bunch of feminist tropes and anti (white) male hatred. It was like the studio made this anti-male revisionist propaganda, and then were SHOCKED that men were not going to see the movie.

The (mostly male) fans of the original felt that the gender swap of the reboot cheapened the original, destroying something great that brought them genuine happiness and joy, to an extent "ruining their childhoods".

Now, besides getting in touch with his feelings, the modern man is supposed to be, above all else, tolerant. He's supposed to be patient with differing viewpoints that he may not understand or appreciate. He's supposed to use empathy and consideration to view things from somebody else's point of view. Agree with it or not, you have to at least concede that the visceral male fan internet backlash was genuine and honest.

So, what happened when men "expressed" their "feelings" about Ghostbusters being remade? Were they treated with the same standard of patience, empathy and understanding that is expected of them? You tell me. On May 28th The Guardian published their interview with female Ghostbuster and movie star Melissa McCarthy:

> *"Ever since the female-led reboot of the beloved 1980s comedy was announced, it has been vilified online, largely by* **manboys** *furious at the idea of estrogen inside the Ghostbuster uniforms. The stars and Feig have been targeted with* **sexist abuse***; notably less trolling has been directed at the male stars of other remakes, such as Jurassic Park or The Karate Kid.*
>
> *All those comments – 'You're ruining my childhood!' I mean, really,"* McCarthy *says drily.* "*Four women doing any movie on earth will destroy your childhood?" She shrugs. "I have a visual of those people not having a Ben [her husband],* **not having friends***, so they're just sitting there and spewing hate into this fake world of the internet. I just hope they* **find a friend***."*

So, there you have it. The Guardian calls the Ghostbusters critics "manboys"; their criticisms were "sexist abuse". According to Melissa McCarthy, any outspoken critic of her movie doesn't have any friends. She was going to accuse her critics of having cooties, but thought that might come off as a little immature.

But, then again, let's try be fair to McCarthy and give her the benefit of the doubt. Let's try to extend some of the compassion and understanding the modern man is always hearing about. I mean maybe she just made a mistake. After all, Hollywood movie stars must do a LOT of interviews.

With that much exposure and attention, I'm sure that it's difficult to always say the right thing at the right time. When you're under a microscope, you're bound to have an off day, make an off-handed comment that you really didn't mean. Something that got misquoted or taken out of context.

And then on June 8th, 2016 when the cast went on Jimmy Kimmel Live, McCarthy had this to say.

> *"What they don't say when they're typing is that one minute after they type their mom is like, 'Get upstairs and take out the garbage! You're 45 years old,'"*

In my humble opinion that was rather petty and uncalled for. First of all, it seems like a socially acceptable way to make fun of poor people. No really, think about it. A 45-year-old male, living in his mother's basement, is basically impoverished. Imagine if she had made fun of homeless people. I guess it's okay to rip on poor people now so long as they have qualms about the feminization of an '80s classic.

Remember too that these critics were FANS of the original. If anything, these people should be in the target audience demographic. They obviously CARE about Ghostbusters, and while that may be hard for some people to understand, the success and popularity of the original was the reason the studio wanted to remake it in the first place. It's why they could justify spending so much money on the production budget, actors' salaries and promotion.

And yet the fiercest of critics could have easily been won over. I mean had she instead said something like:

> *"You know what? I hear these criticisms and I completely understand where they're coming from. To be perfectly honest, I had the same fears before I got the script. To be frank, I get lots of offers for different projects, but when I read how funny this thing was, how it stayed true to the spirit of the original, all of those fears were appeased. I don't blame anybody for being suspicious of a big studio remake of an 80s classic. I would be too. All I ask is that you give it a chance. Because I wouldn't have done it if I didn't know how great it was going to be."*

Of course, she didn't say any of that. I can't speak for everybody, but I know for myself, if I had heard that, I would have been there opening weekend, no question.

Instead McCarthy's obnoxious remarks showed that the cast and crew didn't really care about the fans of the original or their concerns. And it didn't stop there. After a few tweets she didn't like, comedian/actress Leslie Jones lost her sense of humor. She blocked Milo Yiannopoulos from her account, and complained to Twitter to get his account taken down.

A grown woman, a movie star, took time out of her day to limit another human being's free speech because she disagreed with what he was saying.

This controversy is very well documented and discussed extensively online. How the coverage gets framed depends very much on which site you visit.

One point we would like to make is this: If the message of the movie is that women can do everything men can do, or that women don't really NEED men... if all those things are true, then why didn't they just go and create their own successful franchise? The **concept of Ghostbusters** was created by men. The **original Ghostbusters movies** were written and directed by men. The NEW Ghost Busters movie was **directed by a man** (see chapter on Directing Movies).

So, why aren't women making their OWN franchises? If men had taken a movie famous for being all about women, then replaced those women with men, that re-branded co-option would never have been tolerated. Can you imagine a First Husband's Club, or a sequel to Bridesmaids called Groomsmen? Not to mention the reaction if the trailer was filled with anti-female slurs? The real problem with the feminization of Ghostbusters was that it seemed to be PUSHED, not by the popular demand of the public, but by some other politically correct powers-that-be.

Just as controversial as the movie itself was whether or not the reboot was a flop or a success. Jeff Rouner from the Houston Press wrote an article titled, "Ghostbusters Remake Now Officially Not a Flop". On July 18th, Flavorwire posted an article claiming "Pretty Good Movie Does Pretty Good at Box Office" They went on to pair the moderate box office win with the moderate critical success: "So far, 'Ghostbusters' is a modest success -- much like the movie."

So where, oh where, does the truth lie? Was Ghostbusters a flop or a bomb? A mediocre success or a slow moving, gradual train wreck?

See for yourself:
http://thegg.net/articles/paul-feigs-ghostbusters-2016-flops-really-hard-at-the-box-office/

It bombed. It didn't get our money. We saw the preview, and that was more than enough. Could men have gotten excited about a female cast of Ghostbusters? Probably. But the trailer needed to indicate that the women had a healthy view of men.

Remember that, in the original film, Ghostbusters was about 4 guys ghost-busting BUT also expressed an elevated view of women. Bill Murray's love interest in the original Ghostbusters was Dana Barrett (played by Sigourney Weaver). Barrett wasn't a Pamela Anderson type.

She was a sophisticated, seemingly intelligent, woman whom Murray's character was clearly after for more than just her looks. He aspired to be with her, to be viewed well in her eyes. His motivation for success as a Ghostbusters was clearly wrapped up with his desire to woo Barrett.

The original didn't denigrate women, but the reboot

accuses men of being sexist in the trailer!

Also, while none of the original cast were bathing suit models, they weren't obese either. The reboot featured two obese women out of four. If they wanted to have a successful reboot featuring all women Ghostbusters, here is what would have worked:

1. Don't insult men in the trailer.
2. Create a plausible premise why it had to be women ghostbusters (since in reality men do almost all of the dangerous and disgusting jobs - the Ghosts and the Ghostbusting itself should be the only implausible parts of the story).
3. Feature four women who are not obese.
4. I submit to you a premise that combines 1 - 3:
    o the Original cast of the ghostbusters are there in the beginning of the film; they are all counting their money from being famous successful real-life ghostbusters.
    o They all have younger, good-to-fair-looking wives/girlfriends who are not obese. Show the original cast all caught up in the trappings of wealth, Bill Murray (Venkman) lays around in the pool all day sipping margaritas, Egon is geeking out with all the inventions he can buy or make with his dough, Dan Aykroyd (Stantz) has private chefs bringing him every delicacy of food from around the world, and Winston (Ernie Hudson) is impeccably dressed and attending one Hollywood function after another basking in his stylish fame.
    o The wives/girlfriends see a ghost and get slimed. They tell their men, but they are so caught up in the lifestyle that they brush it off. The women decide to take matters into their own hands, find

the old equipment and get busting.

- o That goes fairly well as they learn how to use everything, but at some point things get out of hand. Maybe the men finally wake up out of their fame and fortune stupor when they all get arrested; perhaps all their individual distractions combine into one gathering where things get out of control.
- o From jail they apologize to the women and give them some advice about the equipment and ghost-busting process that they needed at just the right time.
- o The women are then able to conquer the final battle with a little help from their men. This would balance out the focus between the genders in the same way that the Barrett love interest did for the original.
- o One of the men in lock up could use his political pull (since he was so caught up hob knobbing) to remove a political obstacle (*since in the original the EPA and its regulation was one of the antagonists*).

5. If they could figure out how to combine an overheated proton pack with footage of the four good-looking women (to suggest that Ghost-busting just got hotter) all the better.

6. Three out of four of the women should really exemplify femininity with the fourth being a little bit D.U.F.F.[19] just for contrast.

Basically follow the same formula that could have made the WNBA a success (see Chapter 2): don't try to be just like the men, instead show off what people actually love about women. Yes, their beauty and femininity, but also the fact that women sometimes see things that men don't (who have more

---

[19] Designated Ugly Fat Friend

narrowly focused perspectives that help them make so many inventions – *See Chapter 10*) and at times need to step in to fill in where men have a blind spot.

This actually relates back to healthy male-female relationships and does not feed into feminist fantasies. In the original you see Barrett not initially accepting Venkman. She had a standard of what she would accept in a male partner and at the beginning he didn't really match up. It made him a better man that went on to achieve a huge amount and he showed that his interest in her wasn't just a passing fancy. Perfect.

If they would have kept that healthy interchange between the sexes than men would have been fine with a movie where it is the women moving most of the plot along.

This chapter was a little long but we hope we have broken it down so that even feminists and beta-males can understand it.

18 – WOMEN CAN'T BECOME PRESIDENT *(Running Like a Man)*

If you are a feminist that is *just dying* for there to be a woman President, then you should really pay attention here because we actually lay down how a woman could make that happen (by showing you how women can't accomplish this).

We thought we would address this because the whole woman president thing is seen as a sort of glass ceiling. People act like there is some unseen barrier preventing this from happening.

This notion is incredibly flawed because America is not that different from Canada, Germany, the U.K. or any of the Western democracies that have had female leaders.

Also, Female leaders are not a new phenomenon. Queen Elizabeth reigned from the late 1500s to the early 1600s. She ruled for 40 years and during a difficult period in British history.

Beyond that, if you go further back in time, in the post-Greco era there were women who led countries. More recently, take Margaret Thatcher who ruled the UK in the 1980s.

The real problem is that there has not been a qualified female candidate who ran LIKE A WOMAN. If you have a choice between an ACTUAL man and a woman who is PRETENDING to be a man, the voters will pick the real thing.

What do we mean by running like a woman? Well, what did Queen Elizabeth or Margaret Thatcher do that none of the American Presidential candidates have done?

What they did was tap into the "MOTHER ARCHETYPE" in people's minds. Hillary Clinton is doing the soon-to-be-your-ex-wife archetype, harping on things, getting offended easily.

Remember when Carly Fiorina ran, and she got all offended because Trump said something about her face? There is just no way that American voters are going to vote for a female coming at an election from a place of being offended. Coming from the complaining, nagging archetype.

Instead, if American female politicians want the POTUS slot, they need to have this kind of amusement, treating the other candidates as errant children. "Oh, don't worry, mom will take care of everything" kind of thing. That's the energy they need to project, I'm not saying they should actually say that (explaining in case zombie beta-males are reading).

That's exactly the energy that Margaret Thatcher put forth. She never used her womanhood to get her way because that causes men and women to lose respect for you. If you want special treatment because you're a woman, that inherently makes you less respect-worthy (at least in the context being a political leader).

Margaret Thatcher never did that. That said, she knew if she were amused by some liberal attacker and responded with some clever remark that people would view her as a great mother (and not like every woman they ever had a bad relationship with).

See a good mother is never really offended or shocked when you say something stupid. She is amused. After all you are just a child and she is not threatened by you. Therefore, when Thatcher would respond with amusement at some off-color attack made by an opponent it makes them look like little children in the minds of the viewers. What's more, it presents their attack as some childish stupid remark not to be taken seriously.

Can you imagine how Thatcher would have handled a comment about her face? I can't even imagine it but I can tell you it would have been awesome and nothing like Fiorina's lame feigned offense.

That is why Margaret Thatcher was Prime Minister in three consecutive decades and Fiorina was America's briefest ever candidate for the Vice-Presidency.

Similarly, Queen Elizabeth knew she had to tap into that Great Mother archetype. She dressed herself up as Mary, the ultimate mother, the mother of God (according to catholic belief which had just recently been replaced with the Anglo form of Protestantism).

Once you are viewed with a mother's energy, men will do anything for you. Men have that programming to go serve women already in them. Men have no problem serving women. Men have experience following women acting in that mother role (from their childhoods).

Far from being any type of an insult or a judgment call on whether or not a woman SHOULD be president, this chapter should instead be seen as a step-by-step guide, or instruction manual.

Much like Karl Rove telling Obama how to beat Hillary in a WSJ Op-Ed. This is another perspective from the other side of the aisle or "gender spectrum" to put it in zombie PC terminology.

A mini-treatise on what the American people might be looking for and not finding.

The real question then becomes, "Are women capable of running in this way?" Or more to the point, "Are MODERN AMERICAN WOMEN capable of running a campaign in this way?"

Bear in mind, they have grown up with the same masculine-feminine propaganda in schools and TV shows, which all say that the only way for women to be equal to men, is for them to be the SAME as men.

One could see why this doesn't work. For the same reason that Mitt Romney didn't win the presidency. He was a liberal socialist who believed in national healthcare, but why take the pretend lite-version of that when you have the real deal right on the ballot. When there is a lack of differentiation our minds go towards what seems more genuine.

Obama was a more genuine socialist that was more comfortable with himself. Romney could never sell the country on being a real Conservative and he made a really awkward socialist.

This doesn't work for RINOS[20] the same as it does not work for women vying for the highest office using the ex-wife archetype. Well, they are trying to run like a man would run but it just comes off as an ex-wife architype because that is the closest analog in people's mind of when a woman would act like that.

You can't blame us when Hillary loses the 2016 election because we gave you the method that a woman can use to become President. Look, you may not like Trump but the majority of people (probably 70 – 80%) are more amused by Trump than offended.

---

[20] Republicans In Name Only (RINO).

Imagine if we saw Hillary laughing amusedly at the Trump sideshow. Maybe throw in some anecdotes about how she dealt with this kind of behavior with Chelsea – when she was 3 years old!

She needed to laugh with the country. Instead she got offended and it comes off as nagging. Can you imagine a mother getting that upset at a petulant child?

Since she didn't laugh with the country she doesn't look like an amused mother but instead like a pissed off woman. Men are comfortable with women in authority if they view them as mothers. If they view them as wives or girlfriends, then they will be very resistant to being led by them (*Tim Kaine notwithstanding*).

By the way, if you don't think that people process their political leaders by relating to personal relationships they have with people of that gender then you are delusional.

Male politicians are constantly compared to (and processed as) paternal figures, fathers, uncles, husbands and in rare cases male children (cough, Marco Rubio). Female politicians are compared to wives, ex-wives, girlfriends and mothers.

This is why Trump paraded his kids out at the RNC – so the country would view him as a father they wish they'd had. This is why Margaret Thatcher never let any male politician get under her skin – since that would put her in the offended partner light. Someone insults her or says something "sexist" you can just picture her amused smirk (the same smirk a mother would have at her 4-year-old boy saying 'no girls allowed' in their blanket fort – *unless that mother was an evil feminist*).

You can wine about the inequity of it all (like Fiorina did) but you will have similar results, every time. **Embrace the amused mother archetype!**

19 – WOMEN CAN'T DO MATH (AND HARD SCIENCE)

In multiple countries the powers-that-be have really tried to push women into math, technology and science. Both academically and occupationally. Hard science does not usually have to do with interacting with other people or with animals. In sociology, biology and psychology (often referred to as soft sciences) the focus is on people, animals and such.

Women are very well represented in the softer sciences, but if it doesn't involve animals or interpersonal relations, they are not interested in what is called the HARD sciences. Hard sciences are like chemistry, math, engineering, and the other applied sciences.

Society has tried to push women into these fields, from schooling to scholarships and so on, and women by and large just resist it. I often wondered why people felt this need to force women to do things they are just not inclined to do.

Now to be fair and balanced, here is a mentally ill blogger pontificating about how sexism is keeping women out of science (which is complete nonsense):
http://www.businessinsider.com/7-things-keeping-women-out-of-science-2013-10

You can read her nonsensical rantings if you wish, but let's breakdown her 7 main points here. These are the reasons she gives for why there aren't more women scientists and technologists (*only childcare has some legitimacy but you have to go complain to nature on that one*) and our response to each one:

1. **Teasing in school** - *are you kidding me? You don't think any male science nerds were teased before it became cool to be a geek?*
2. **Lack of encouragement** - *PLEASE! This suggests that the men that achieved in the field of science did so because someone coddled them with an encouraging embrace. The reality is this: it is a **biological imperative for men to be able to generate resources**. Millions of women get married without ever having to work. Even if*

they do have some nonsense job guys just don't care about it (for the most part). So, throughout the centuries **if you didn't have brawn** *you had to* **generate resources with your brains.** *The men that didn't were (for the most part) weeded out of the gene pool. Plus, as we will get to, men and women have different priorities from the moment they are born (before any "socialization" can take place).*

3. **Stereotypes** - *hmmmm, I wonder if there are any negative stereotypes about male nerds... In fact, there were so many they made a movie series called "Revenge of the Nerds". Why did they need revenge? If anything the stereotype of the girl nerd is that she is sought after and desired by male geeks the world over.*

4. **Childcare** - biologically men simply cannot carry unborn children, birth them, recover and breastfeed them for the requisite 18 months that follow, SORRY!

5. **Competition** - *I scarcely know what to say about this one. If you can't handle the competition in a field, then you by definition do not deserve a spot in that field.*

6. **Marginalization** - made up feminist word, NEXT!

7. **Bias** - okay, I'm done with this list - I've patronized this female blogger long enough.

Basically, everything this list boils down to the same thing: it's **the worlds fault that women aren't achieving** in this particular field.

Now the next article that addresses this subject is a little better. While I don't agree with everything she says, Denise Cummins is in the ball park in her article "Why the STEM gender gap is overblown"[21]. My favorite is her response to this idea that girls are born a "blank slate" and "socialized" into picking certain fields of work.

The problem with this "blank slate" interpretation of gender differences is that it doesn't jive with results of developmental studies.

---

[21] http://www.pbs.org/newshour/making-sense/truth-women-stem-careers/

Newborn girls prefer[22] to look at faces while newborn boys prefer to look at mechanical stimuli (such as mobiles). When it comes to toys, a consistent finding is that boys (and juvenile male monkeys) strongly prefer to play with mechanical toys over plush toys or dolls, while girls (and female juvenile monkeys) show equivalent interest in the two. (See this for summary[23] of this research.) These sex-linked preferences emerge in human development long before any significant socialization can have taken place. And they exist in juvenile non-human primates that are not exposed to human gender-specific socialization efforts.

It is not difficult to see how such early emerging preferences can end up shaping career choices later on; women tend to gravitate toward fields that focus on living things and agents, men to fields that focus on objects and abstract concepts.

---

[22] http://www.math.kth.se/matstat/gru/5b1501/F/sex.pdf

[23] http://www.ncbi.nlm.nih.gov/pmc/articles/PMC2583786/#%21po=7.14286 – *yummy rhesus monkeys, I want to love 'em to pieces!*

As a side note, the more women vote, and the more they completely control education, the worse it gets. Especially in fields like math, recent Common Core changes have made it so students still get credit for getting math questions wrong as long as they can "show work".

That is very female. The male mind says, "well in the real world if I do crap work then no one will care about my so-called work".

What else do we pretend women can do that they really can't? Oh yeah! (See next chapter)

20 – WOMEN CAN'T GO TO (REAL) WAR

While women pretend to teach kids math with programs like common core, other women are pretending to be soldiers.

Look we are going to keep this short and sweet. No data is needed because these truths be self-evident.

Women waited for thousands of years before they attempted to become soldiers (*in any large numbers – for the generalization police if you are reading*).

I wonder why, all of a sudden, they are willing to don a uniform and enlist... could it possibly be that now being a soldier in the west is **safer than being a fisherman**? I mean now that there are so many office and button-pushing jobs in the military it is kind of nice (once the benefits are thrown in). Plus, if things get too hairy they can always get pregnant and get discharged.

You may not like what I'm saying but you can't change that these are facts. You can't go back in time and change the fact that women enjoyed the privilege to not get drafted for millennia.

The fact is that female life has always been regarded as more valuable than male life (*since after all one man can happily do the job of 20 or 30 in terms of impregnating women to keep the species going, whereas if 75% of the women died the other 25% would have a real hard time making up for the lost population*).

Even today, if women in the armed forces were dying at any significant rate society would not put up with it.

Kind of amazing that after WWI ended in 1918 where millions of drafted men had spilt their blood in horrific battle, just a few years later, women in most western countries were granted the privilege to vote without taking on the associated obligations, namely of being subject to the draft.

Also, women were given an equal vote even though their tax contributions were almost non-existent (and are still net-zero – See Chapter 3).

Feminism has essentially followed this template since then. I speak of the template of fighting for increased *privileges* for women without adding to their associated responsibility (*and in some cases reducing their obligations as in the case of alimony and welfare payments where **they get** what they want from men **without having to give** anything in return*).

Where were the women soldiers when soldiering meant being mustard gassed, getting limbs sawed off without anesthetic, and nearly freezing to death in trenches while trying to screw on their bayonets?

Women avoided all that because the patriarchy was oppressing them from dying en mass? Do you really believe that?

That is ridiculous. The reality is that men have always given women what they wanted, maybe not immediately but at least within a generation. This is because the women raise the children (hence they teach the next generation).

In fact, polling indicated that the more women opposed female suffrage than men[24].

Women only got behind the idea of being granted a vote[25] when it became clear that it would not come with the associated obligation of being subject to the draft.

---

[24]
http://www.oxfordscholarship.com/view/10.1093/acprof:oso/9780199248773.001.0001/acprof-9780199248773

[25] As a side note, women were NOT oppressed by not having the vote. Only men could vote because they bore the cost of government – both in blood and gold. http://www.avoiceformen.com/feminism/feminist-lies-feminism/women-were-not-oppressed-by-not-having-the-vote/

21 – WOMEN CAN'T MOVE *(Without Men's Help)*

Why are you here? No, but really though. How did you get here? YOU'RE not moving. You HATE moving. Nah, but like your friend's friend is moving *(maybe he is trying to date her so you are **proxy simping**)*. She doesn't know your name; you barely know hers. But you're here now.

For a while. Like a LONG time. Like an amount of time that has no end. This is your day now. Your whole day, and you don't even know this person, or particularly like this person. The more you get to know her, the more you regret agreeing to this.

He-Haul!

You get the large stuff first. Straighten the back and stand, so you're lifting with the legs, not the back. She's got the blender. This woman is carrying a blender. It's almost like the larger the things YOU carry, the smaller the items she gets.

You don't care if the stuff ends up in a dumpster or set on fire, at this point, but for some unknowable reason you are still taking great care with these obtuse objects that you can barely squeeze through the stairwell (because of course her building has no elevator).

"Be careful with that. It's a this-or-a-that. it's just, hmmm... okay. Ummm... Maybe if you just-"

"WHAT? Maybe if I just WHAT? Maybe if YOU just

hired moving men, I wouldn't be here, that MAYBE?"

***

"Oh my Gooodddness. I... love... This place... Is that mahogany?"

You don't love this place. **You hate this place** and you hate the mahogany. You hate all places and all things and all types of wood that have a name.

At this point you are starving. Everyone is starving (by everyone I mean the girl moving, her friend whose main job seems to be talking with the girl who's moving, and the 4 other guys she has roped into being her day-slaves).

You and the rest of the guys have formed an ad-hoc inconspicuous support group. You give each other the look; maybe you gripe quietly about the heat, how long it is taking, how the chick didn't even have everything packed up when you got there to move her, and most of all about when is the food going to show up.

What food are we talking about? You know the free food that **any decent person would be providing** to a group of random men that agreed to be your moving servants for the day. Eventually someone actually has to tell the girl moving that there is an implicit understanding that she is required to feed people providing free moving services.

Of course, she planned out JUST ENOUGH money to pay for the moving van and the tape gun she failed to foresee needing. So she gets pizza. Rather A PIZZA. ONE (1) PIZZA for everyone. After all there is you, 4 other guys she roped into this, the girl moving and her worthless friend. So 7 people + 8 slices = MORE than enough.

That's using crazy lady math of course (see Chapter 19 - "Women Can't Do Math").

When it is all said and done, she, sort of, half-thanks everyone. By this late in the day any response seems like a lie.

- **"Your welcome"**: welcome to what? Welcome to ask me to do this again? **HELL NO.**
- **"No problem"**: it was a **HUGE PROBLEM**. If you are planning to live for a lot longer you have to tell yourself that no future day will be as bad as today.
- **"No worries"**: she really should be worried... about a **lot of things**. Mainly how to save $1000 so she can pay movers if she ever moves again. Either that or marry some guy who has a $1000 so he can pay the movers, or just figure something out <u>not</u> involving you.

Your new motto is the same as the JDL (or Jewish Defense League): NEVER AGAIN! NEVER AGAIN!

22 – WOMEN CAN'T AGE WITH DIGNITY

YouTube Makeup channels, plastic surgery, Spanx, liposuction, creams made from crushed pearls... none of it turns back time, nor should it.

Aging is a way of nature being honest with men at large about their chances of continuing their genetic lineage with the woman in question. By their 40's women should be enjoying their newfound grandma-hood, not trying to pick up dudes at the Blue Martini.

After a woman's mid-20s her fertility (likelihood of being able to conceive and birth a child) begins its steady decline. At around age 35 a woman's fertility drops rapidly and the chances for birth defects climbs just as quickly.

Why is fertility so important? What about guys not looking to have kids? The reality is that our attraction is based on continuing our genes. We think a chick is "hot" because she is showing signs of fertility and femininity.

It is not shallow for guys to like breasts that are ample but not too big (and also not saggy). It isn't some pointless aesthetic preference. Small breasted women have trouble breastfeeding. People with no breasts might be men. If they are too big then either the woman is obese or she has some deformity (usually the former).

Obesity correlates with infertility so again this is just a rational preference that is based on a man's chance of continuing his genes on beyond his death. Again saggy breasts are usually an indicator of advanced age which correlates with infertility.

So the reason why women are having such a hard time aging with dignity is that they haven't used their fertility rationally in their younger years.

By contrast, when my wife makes it into her 40's we will have had and (pretty much) raised all of our three kids. The oldest will likely be starting her family and we will be looking forward to being there for our grandkids. At that point what purpose would my wife have in getting done up to look like she is still a teenager and head to the local nightclub (with favorable lighting)?

At that point she will have already used her valuable eggs rationally and given me 3 wonderful kids that she has already finished weening and raising. Beyond our own love for each other we have kids, and then grand kids, that we will need to guide as long as we are alive. That increases the strength of our bond to each other. Therefore, she will not be threatened by younger women because she used her youth rationally. **That is aging with dignity**.

Most women today are putting off having children until the last possible moment and when they finally get around to it many of them are finding out it is too late. Clubbing may have been fun in their teenage years and through most of their 20's. But with those years squandered what type of men are going to want to pick them up in their late 30's (not to mention their 40's or 50's)?

Not any rational man that wants to start a family. So they usually pick up some beta-male that has no concern for his own genetic lineage. Usually they've picked up a kid or two that they often can't trace back to a credible father. As the expression goes, Alpha lays and Beta pays.

Eventually these women get sick of their Beta-male man-pets and dump them. Then they get out all the trickery they have accumulated over the years (makeup/Spanx/etc) and try and fool some unsuspecting guy into thinking there are some fresh eggs still around. Usually the eggs have dried up into unusable powdered eggs.

> **SIDE NOTE**: By the way, even if a guy has no interest at all in having kids his genes still do. If that weren't the case, why aren't these guys all chasing single women in their 60's? I mean you don't even need to worry about protection (pregnancy wise).
>
> Obviously even if you have some mental hang up about the responsibility of raising kids (even though someone did it for you) you are still biologically programmed to chase after fertility markers.

Needless to say, this whole process is anything but Aging with Dignity.

23 – WOMEN CAN'T GET READY QUICKLY

You're ready. You've already been ready already. There's an episode of Ed, Edd n' Eddy on TV, which you haven't seen since you were a wee little seedling. It provides some tranquility and stress relief to this PTSD you're feeling (or PETDSD).

You discussed and decided on an ETD, she KNOWS when you're supposed to be there, and (by extension) when you're supposed to leave. It started gradually actually, like she made small talk for kind of a long time and seemed to lack urgency.

She asked you what you thought of this top, that dress and something called a pashmina. Is it too much or too little? Does it make a part of her body seem larger or smaller than it actually is? She doesn't want people to get the wrong or right idea about anything.

You answered half-thinking really: "Yeah, great, wonderful, fantastic. Are you ready? Like really ready? Can we go now, please?"

"Oh, I can't believe you. You'll say anything's pretty because you just wanna leave."

Which is true, I suppose. So really, you should have started out critical. You should have picked something apart, like an early outfit. You should have been cruel from the start. Should've called her first outfit plain old plain and old, and ugly. That way you'd have some credibility when you love a later outfit and want to leave.

What world is this? It's absurd. It's ridiculous. You start out nice at first, calm and polite, something like, "I told them such and such" or "we're supposed to be there by this and that"... "I wanted to beat the traffic, but now I wanna beat people, but I can't because that's frowned upon and illegal."

You're already late. Somehow, someway you're late BEFORE you're late, because that's how traffic and sequential occurrence work, so now you're late twice and she's not even sorry once.

You break down and call your friend to give him the heads up. "What'd he say?"

"He said 'that's fine, don't worry about it.'"

"See, there you go."

"Um no, there we don't go. We're still here. He said 'not to worry about it' to be a nice person, because he IS a nice person, which is why I'm friends with him in the first place. I wanna be a nice person as well... which is why I wanted to be on time. Because other people exist. Like my nice friend, whom I wanted to be on time for. I'll be in the car!"

But then you're just burning gasoline... Listening to A.M. radio, which isn't as good at night as it is in the afternoon. You have no eyes on her progression, so you're forced to speculate. If you just knew HOW late you were going to be BEFORE being that late, then maybe you could set your expectations, limit your trepidation, breathe in, face it, exhale and embrace it.

She gets in the car, closes the door and opens the mirror for her make up. There's excuses, consternation, an insincere apology with a side of equivocation. Somehow she's mad at you for being mad at her. Is this communication? She's defensive, she's never wrong. If she can't change, she just might be single and walking home by the end of the night (and not your home).

24 – WOMEN CAN'T MAKE COMIC BOOKS

Think of every famous comic book hero or superhero that you can right now. From Superman to Batman, X-Men, and so on down the line. They all have one thing in common. Whether they are DC or Marvel or Dark Horse, they were all created by MEN. Comic books have seen a resurgence of late at the box office, some of these movies -- like the Dark Night and The Avengers -- grossing over a billion dollars.

All of these comic books, from their characters, to their artistic renderings, to their story lines, settings and villains were ALL created by men. What is somewhat ironic is that even the famous female super heroes, which there are not as many of, Super Girl, Catwoman, Bat Girl, Wonder Woman, were nevertheless created by men.

This is seen as a problem by the people who monitor diversity in things, like it is due to some type of discrimination. NPR was trying to make us feel bad about there not being more minority super heroes. All I could think of was, "everybody has access to printing presses."

If you want to get a comic made, put your money where your mouth is, and produce a comic. If you have some great minority super hero, go for it. If you want an Afghani non-terrorist superhero, great! Go make it. Or in terms of women, if women made comics about female superheroes, and people WANTED to buy those comics... there would BE those comics.

It's funny to go through any list of female comic creators, because most of the names are colorists. But as far as the people who actually created the comics, there is hardly any created by women, or if they were any I haven't heard of them. Like Phantom Lady. Have YOU ever heard of Phantom Lady? No, of course not. If Phantom Lady isn't a great comic, or a popular one, it's not OUR fault, but we get blamed for it.

As far as other forms of supposed discrimination, why women might not be getting promoted as easily or as often as men do, comic books -- at least from the 1930s through to the 1970s when you were still seeing new, successful characters get created and become popular, they were essentially all created by entrepreneurs, people who started their own companies (like Stan Lee).

There really was no corporation or infrastructure that was preventing women from creating their own independently successful comic book characters.

Even as late as the 1970s, Teenage Mutant Ninja Turtles was started by 2 guys in a dingy apartment. The Watchmen was created in the 1970s by one man, alone. One can hardly argue that the success of these comic books is due to some male-dominated, chauvinistic discrimination preventing females from creating strong female comic books and getting them into the hands of female comic book readers.

Further Reading:
NPR trying to make me feel bad:
http://www.npr.org/sections/codeswitch/2014/01/11/261449394/who-gets-to-be-a-superhero-race-and-identity-in-comics
My Response: Nothing is stopping minorities, women, foreigners and the disabled from making comics (by the way I am in at least two minority groups myself).

Exhaustive list of women "involved" with comic books:

https://en.wikipedia.org/wiki/List_of_female_comics_creators

25 – WOMEN CAN'T UNDERSTAND GENERALIZATIONS (Generally Speaking)

Feminists, social justice warriors, brain-dead beta-males, and politically correct zombies – we warned you at the beginning that you weren't going to understand this book.

We explained that "you lot" have a hard time understanding what is meant by generalizations. You have this habit of interpreting general comments as a universalization.

Of course, your lot can make all the generalizations it wants as long as it is about men, white people, westerners, people with different views on politics or economics.

The Head Feminazi (Hillary Clinton) just recently made a generalized comment about Trumps supporters, saying they were a "basket of deplorables" and that they were largely "irredeemable". I didn't expect to ever see the DNC Nominee for President condemn half of all Americans to eternal damnation. Higher taxes and less free speech, sure.

Even though we warned you about generalizations we still tried to make mention of it throughout the book with parenthetical statements like "(generally speaking)" and such. This was because we tried to make this easy enough for even feminists and beta-males to understand.

We hope we didn't confuse you too much. We hope you were able to handle us discussing the **Stuff Women Can't Do**. Again, we deeply respect the women in our life and they loved what we put together here.

Remember this book is not anti-women in the slightest (as much as you would love to brand it that way). Instead it is just opening up an honest conversation about what men uniquely bring to the table (by pointing out the **Stuff Women Can't Do)**.

Everyone already understands what women can do that men can't – most amazingly the ability to create new human beings and then automatically go into dairy production to produce exactly what that new life needs to eat when it is born. As a father that was there seeing my daughter be born I can say that is truly amazing.

Men can't come close to women in that regard. We sincerely hope that you enjoyed learning about the areas of life where men shine. We hope you are mature enough to take this book for what it is and if you really think we got something wrong that you email us or give us some constructive reviews.

For the love of all that is good about Amazon reviews: we beg you not to comment that there are exceptions to the generalizations we make in this book. That will just make you look ridiculous to the people that actually read and understood this volume.

With that we leave you with a bonus honorable mention that didn't make the list. That's right, there is some more Stuff Women Can't Do and we are going to end on a real fun note.

HONORABLE MENTION: Women Can't Appreciate Monty Python

Your girlfriend does not really like Monty Python. She just doesn't get it. She might like you and by extension watch and even occasionally laugh at Monty Python. "Oh but this girl I dated totally liked Monty Python and the Holy Grail" you may say. Alright, maybe she enjoyed their most widely acclaimed movie "a bit, yeah, a bit".

But, really, no women really appreciate Monty Python. To truly appreciate it you have to enjoy hours of Monty Python's Flying Circus. It just isn't happening guys. If they seem to be really into it she is just trying to be into what you are into – which isn't the end of the world either. You will be watching your share of chick flicks down the road so enjoy it while it lasts!

It is distinctly male humor. Can you picture a comparable female comedy team coming up with something like the Ministry of Silly Walks? Not happening.

Not The Minister Of Silly Walks

Let's get a woman's viewpoint on this. **Jodi Ambrose**, author of *"Intimacy: How to Get More of It: A peek into understanding the male mind"* had this to say on her blog:

> *My thought is that women suffer through Monty Python to bond with their man, not out of an undying love for it. This came up the other day with the hubby and he was horrified that I'd ever say such a thing. After all, isn't Monty Python the funniest thing on planet earth?*
>
> *While I realize the answers to these questions may be different for people in the UK (yes, Mondrak, YOU!) I have to know these things:*
>
> 1. *Ladies, do you really really like Monty Python or have you suffered in silence while your man passes out with laughter?*
> 2. *Gentlemen, what makes you love MP so much???? WHAT??? I NEED TO KNOW.*

I couldn't have said it better myself, although perhaps with less consecutive punctuation marks.

As far as me being able to explain why we love MP so much, that is like trying to get a man excited about buying a china hutch: just not going to happen.

FURTHER READING

SECTION 1: WHEN PROSECUTORS ATTACK!

When Prosecutors Attack is about three innocent men and the governmental-media complex that turned against them.

NEW TRAYVON MARTIN INFO: This explosive new book on the Trayvon Martin case exposes the remarkable story **behind** the stolen jewelry that puts this entire case in a whole new light. Also, we breakdown the so called **"Black Zimmerman"** Roderick Scott case and revisit the trial of the century OJ Simpson case to see what connections can be made to George Zimmerman.

FIND OUT!
Is Roderick Scott the "Black Zimmerman" (As Some Have Claimed)?
FIND OUT!
Do Prosecutors Really **Bribe Witnesses**?
FIND OUT!
What Goes Wrong with High Profile Cases?
FIND OUT!
The Truth About **OJ Simpson** (And Why You Should Care)!
FIND OUT!
Was Trayvon Martin a Drug Dealer (As Some Have Claimed)?
FIND OUT!
Is the Media Trying to Start a **Race War**?

https://www.amazon.com/Niles-Mercado/e/B017GSE62G/

REMEMBER! You never know who will be
next *WHEN PROSECUTORS ATTACK!!!*

NILES MERCADO

SECTION 2: BUSH KILLING REAGAN

George Bush Sr. had the most to gain from President Reagan's death. To hide or conceal his involvement in the assassination attempt George Bush would have to either suppress or lie about his close ties with the shooter and the second gunman hiding on the roof (or "Bushy Knoll"). The story of **BUSH KILLING REAGAN** is so depraved that it is no wonder the story has never been told before.

FIND OUT - Why NBC reported a second gunman!

FIND OUT - Why Reagan was shot by order of his own Vice-President!

FIND OUT - Was George Bush Sr. Friends with Reagan's would-be assassin?

FIND OUT - Why Hinckley's gun didn't match the bullet!

FIND OUT - Was Hinckley a victim of CIA mind control?

FIND OUT - How Reagan's Presidency changed AFTER the shooting!

FIND OUT - How the Trilateral Commission finally infiltrated Reagan's Cabinet! What else weren't we told in this sick and twisted tale of **BUSH KILLING REAGAN?**

http://amzn.com/B019R3OFMO

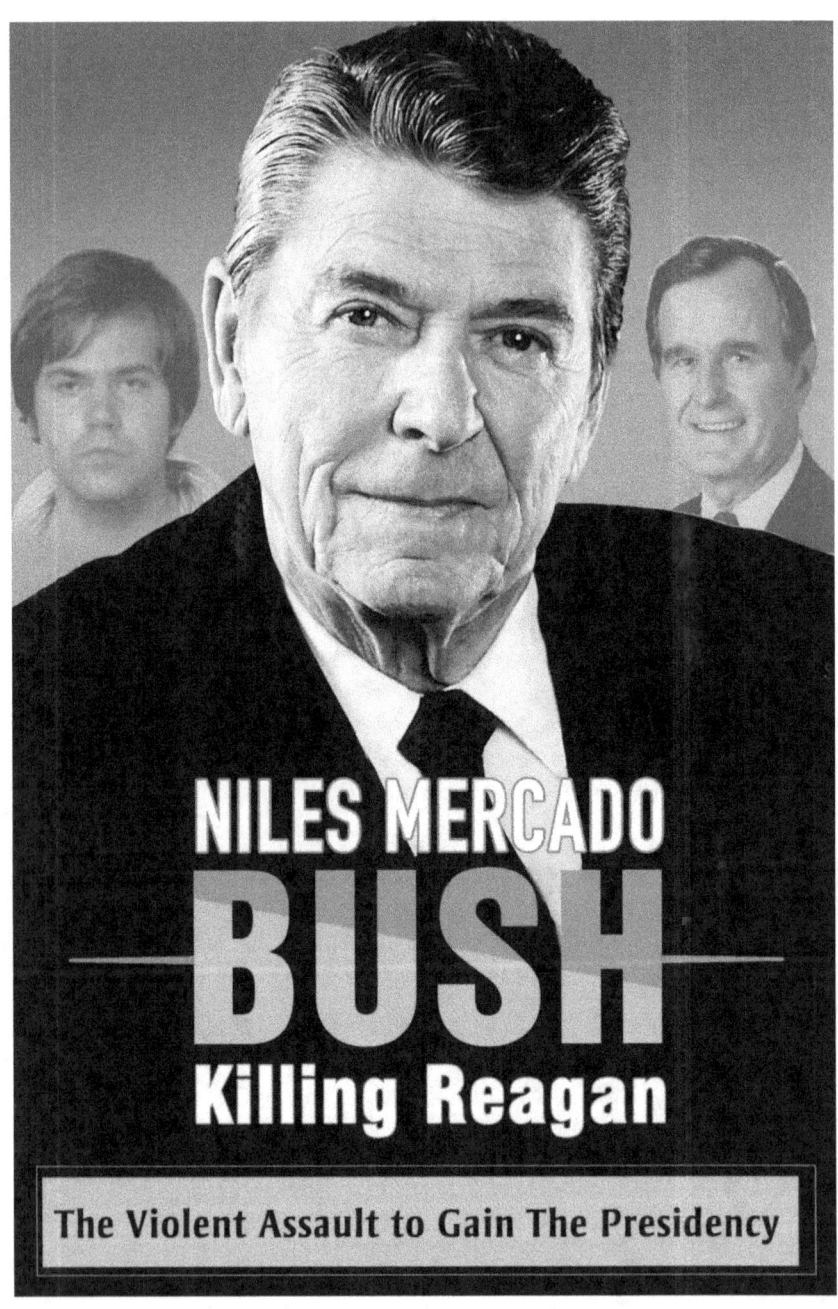

FREE GIFT SPECIAL REPORT
The Tidiest and Messiest Places on Earth

One thing women can definitely is keep things clean! We made a special report about the Tidiest and Messiest Places on Earth! This report is a great supplement to that summary that is all about the virtues of being tidy.

As our **free gift** for being a **MERCADO** enthusiast we are happy to give you a special report about the **3 Most Messy** and the **3 Most Tidy** places on Earth.

Learn about everything from **Garbage Island** to Computer-Chip **Clean Rooms** (and, of course, everything in between).

Get your **free copy** at:

http://sixfigureteen.com/messy

ALSO: We will let you know about future **SUMMARY** titles so this is **win-win**! Our publisher has multiple brands for putting out summaries of the latest books on the Best-Sellers list. Enjoy your **FREE GIFT** and thank you for being part of the **MERCADO** Family!

FREE GIFT SPECIAL REPORT

The 10 Strange Deaths of Vladimir Putin

It may be hard for people to accept that American politicians at times try and get political opponents killed for their own purposes because we live among those same politician's marketing and propaganda. Often it is easier to examine other countries more objectively than our own.

As our **free gift** for being a **STUFF WOMEN CAN'T DO enthusiast** we are happy to give you a special report about some of the mysterious and <u>strange deaths</u> that have befallen Mr. Putin's enemies.

Plane crashes, multiple stab wounds and radioactive sushi are just a few of the misfortunes that have opposed the Russian President.

Get your free copy at:

http://sixfigureteen.com/putinreport